FRED ASTAIRE

ROY PICKARD

Crescent Books

New York

Photographic acknowledgments

Culver Pictures, New York, 10; Frank Driggs Collection, New York, 12, 15, 17, 26, 40 top and bottom, 41, 42 bottom, 46, 52, 54 top, 55, 56 top, 57, 58 bottom, 59, 60, 62, 65, 66 bottom, 68–9, 70, 73, 75, 76 top and bottom, 79, 81, 86, 87 top and bottom, 89, 94, 99, 102, 110, 111, 113, 115, 119, 121, 124, 130, 134 top, 135, 136, 137, 138, 140 top, 142, 143, 146, 151, 153, 160, 182 top and bottom; Lester Glassner Collection, New York, 9, 14, 16, 18, 20, 24–5, 31, 36, 37, 38, 44 bottom, 49, 162, 163, 164–5, 166 bottom, 167, 168 top, 170, 183; Illustrated London News Picture Library, London, 13, 19; The Kobal Collection, London, 7, 8, 11, 21, 23, 27, 28–9, 30, 32, 33, 34 top and bottom, 39, 43, 44 top, 45, 47, 50–1, 53, 54 bottom, 56 bottom, 58 top, 61 top and bottom, 63, 64, 66 top, 67, 71, 74, 77, 78 top and bottom, 80 top and bottom, 82–3, 84 top and bottom, 85, 88 top and bottom, 90, 91, 92, 93, 96–7, 98, 100, 101, 103, 105, 106–7, 112, 114, 116–7, 118, 120, 122–3, 125, 126, 127, 128 top and bottom, 129, 131, 133, 134 bottom, 139, 140 bottom, 141, 144 top and bottom, 145, 148–9, 150, 152 top and bottom, 154, 156–7, 158, 166 top, 168 bottom, 169, 171, 172–3, 174, 175, 177, 178–9, 180, 181, 184 bottom; The Photo Source/Keystone Press, London, 109; Popperfoto, London, 35, 42 top, 108, 176, 184 top; Rex Features, London, 185

Frontispiece: Fred Astaire in the mid-1950s as Daddy Long Legs, the only musical he made for Twentieth Century Fox, 1955. (The Kobal Collection, London)

First English edition published by
Deans International Publishing
52–54 Southwark Street, London SE1 1UA
A division of The Hamlyn Publishing Group Limited
London · New York · Sydney · Toronto

This 1985 edition is published by Crescent Books
Distributed by Crown Publishers, Inc.

Library of Congress Cataloging in Publication Data
Pickard, Roy.
  Fred Astaire.
  Filmography: p.
  1. Astaire, Fred.
  2. Dancers—United States—Biography.
  I. Title.
GV1785.A83P53 1985   793.3'2'0924 [B]   84-29239
ISBN 0-517-45804-7

Printed in Spain

FRED ASTAIRE

CONTENTS

LET'S DANCE

Fred Astaire once commented: 'When I see myself on the screen I'm immediately sorry about the whole business. I want to get up and walk out. And I sometimes do.'

In the 50-plus years he's been singing and dancing (and acting) on the screen he is, in all probability, one of the very few who *has* walked out of one of his movies. Most people have stayed in their millions to watch a man who, by general consent, is the greatest song and dance entertainer of the century.

Possessed of a voice that America's most celebrated composers have queued up to write for – a shy, graceful and always likeable presence, an inimitable little swagger walk and twinkling feet that have danced to more than 180 musical numbers in over 50 years in movies – he was and is an original. Producers had only to give him a tune, an idea and a prop and he would invariably come up with something magical. He has danced with shoes that came alive, brought an amusement arcade to sparkling life, performed with a hat-stand, even, when given half the chance, danced on the ceiling.

Irving Berlin has maintained that he would rather Fred Astaire sang his songs than anyone else. Rudolf Nureyev has called him 'an inspiration'. To the late George Balanchine he was 'the greatest dancer in the world' and Bing Crosby once said: 'There never was, nor ever will be, a better dancer.'

The following pages pay tribute to Fred Astaire, song and dance man. Rather, they pay tribute to Fred Astaire, *screen* song and dance man, an entertainer who began his film career at the height of the depression in 1933. It was then that Fred took a long, sometimes hazardous and frequently rickety journey by a Ford tri-motor plane to Los Angeles and, 'wide-eyed and open-mouthed' risked all on an uncertain future.

But, before that point is reached, a prelude must be included to sketch in something of the early years of the man who was to become a household name all over the world by exploring the whole scope of dance and raising tap dancing to an elegant art. And it must be included because when Fred arrived in Hollywood he was already 34, old for a dancer. He arrived as a star of both the New York and London stage where he had danced to enor-mous popular acclaim in a long series of musicals with his sister Adele.

Broadway success, however, as others had already discovered, was no guarantee of film stardom and when Fred made the trip to Holly-wood, he had the uncomfortable feeling that his best years, his great days with Adele, were already behind him. As for the movies? Well, they at least offered new opportunities and the chance to broaden his horizons. And, with talkies firmly established, they were obviously the medium of the future. But Fred, approaching his mid-30s, didn't look to the future with any great confidence. Just the opposite in fact. He wondered about the days ahead with more than a little trepidation. . . .

It all began in Omaha, Nebraska, on 10 May 1899, when Fred was born, the second child of Frederick and Ann Austerlitz.

Fred's father was an Austrian immigrant. A former officer in the Imperial army, he had found life in his native Vienna not very much to his liking and, like thousands of other Europeans, travelled to find a new life in the States. Just a year after arriving in America he met and married a young school-teacher, then still in her teens, named Ann Gelius.

Frederick's first job was working in a leather shop, which he didn't much care for. His second was as a salesman in the brewery business which was much more interesting and at which he made quite a successful living. At heart, he was some-thing of a frustrated musician and performer. He played the piano, loved music and the theatre and was full of stories about the old days in Vienna, frequently telling young Fred that there were only two kinds of Austrian, rascals and musicians. He never left Fred in any doubt that he very definitely belonged in the latter category.

Most accounts of Fred's early career pinpoint the time he first became interested in dancing as the afternoon he was taken by his mother to pick up his sister Adele (one and a half years his senior) from one of her lessons at the Chamber's Dancing Academy on Omaha's West Farnum Street. Adele, who was so talented a dancer that she was regarded as something of a child prodigy, had first been enrolled at the school at the age of four and was

thought to have a promising future by her teacher.

As he sat on the bench outside the hall, waiting for his mother to return with Adele, Fred noticed two discarded ballet slippers lying nearby. Interested to see if he too could stand on his toes like the girls in Adele's class, he laced them round his feet and found that he could indeed stand on his toes. Fred himself doesn't give much credence to the story (although as he was only six he would be hard put to remember it) and it may well be that it's one of those stories that has become embroidered more with fantasy than fact as it has been passed down over the years.

But the upshot was that it wasn't long afterwards that Fred and Adele began dancing together and not long after that that the pair of them were taken to New York by their mother in the hope that she would find the beginnings of a career for them in vaudeville.

Fred's father stayed behind in Omaha and earned the money for their keep, visiting them in New York as often as he could. Fred's mother had the thankless task of touring the seedy offices of agents and trying to discover if there was indeed any chance for her two children in the rough, tough world of show business.

All the time she kept them on their toes by enrolling them at Claude Alvienne's Dancing School on Eighth Avenue. Alvienne was a kind man who gave her and the children every encouragement but Ann Austerlitz needed all the resources at her command to stay on in New York. The city was not exactly short of mothers who believed their children to be God's gift to the theatre. Competition was tough, to say the least. Most of the mothers were quickly disillusioned and made their way back to their homes in small-town America, their dreams gone forever. Not Ann Austerlitz. She kept hanging on, believing all the time that her children really did have that extra something. Whether she thought that about both Fred *and* Adele isn't clear. Adele, she believed, had always been the one with the true talent. Fred was OK but most people who saw him felt that it didn't go much further than that. Indeed, Fred himself later remarked: 'I only started to dance in 1906 because my sister Adele did. I literally followed in her footsteps. I just went along for the ride.'

Fred with one of his most unusual dancing 'partners' – a hat rack in a scintillating dance sequence from MGM's Royal Wedding *(1951).*

8

Fred pictured with Adele on her twelfth birthday. The pair were already 'veterans' of the vaudeville circuit!

That ride eventually led to a small town in New Jersey called Keyport. It was there that Fred and Adele first danced together in a professional engagement. The booking had been arranged through the kind auspices of Claude Alvienne who shared their mother's enthusiasm for their talents. Their billing was 'Juvenile Artists Presenting an Electric Musical Toe-dancing Novelty'. They played a miniature bride and groom in full evening-dress and danced on and around two colossal wedding cakes to the 'Dreamland Waltz'. Fred was seven, Adele nine. It was the first time that Fred wore top hat, white tie and tails!

The theatres such as the one in Keyport were known as try-out theatres in those days. The audiences were tough. One aged vaudevillian referred to the women who sat in the front rows as 'mothers who ate their young'. But on the night that Fred and Adele made their début the toughness went out of the audience. The women in the front row did not eat them. They took them to their hearts as did the rest of the audience. The local theatre critic wrote: 'The Astaires are the greatest act in vaudeville.'

Shortly afterwards Frank Vincent also saw their potential and booked them into a tour on the famous Orpheum Circuit. They were lined up for 20 weeks at $150 a week. The cost of transport was thrown in.

It seemed like the beginning of one of those

Fred and Adele in The Passing Show of 1918 *which ran for 125 performances at Broadway's Winter Garden Theatre. The pair sang five Sigmund Romberg/Jean Schwartz songs including 'Quick Service' and 'I Can't Make My Feet Behave'.*

movie biography successes with scenes of trains flying towards the screen accompanied by the names of the towns through which they passed and billboards showing the names of the two Astaires – Fred and Adele – getting larger and larger as they worked their way up the bill.

It didn't quite happen like that. The next five years were full of heart-break, disillusion, tough times, rough times. Fred and Adele did all right for a bit but then the novelty of their act began to wear off and they had to find a new one. The new routine didn't always hit the mark. The four of them, for Fred's father had now joined them as manager, needed all their willpower to keep going. It was a life lived in seedy boarding houses and hotels and full of long arduous train journeys and empty stations and half-empty theatres. They shared their lives with jugglers, clowns and acrobats, all of whom were part of their vaudeville world. Some were hoping for the break into the big time. Most were on their way to nowhere having been nowhere. Fred wrote later: 'We travelled every rat trap and chicken coop in the middle west.'

A combination of luck, tenacity, humour and talent saw the Astaires through, especially Adele, who for all the time she worked on stage, strove to improve her dancing skills. As indeed did Fred but with him it was often a case of having to, simply to keep up with his talented sister, for most people agreed that it was Adele who carried the act.

After a two-year break when bookings fell away, the children went to a non-theatrical school in New Jersey and served another period at a New York dancing school. Then it was back on the circuit and this time things at last began to pick up.

The break-through years were 1916 and 1917. The former marked their farewell to vaudeville, the latter their début on Broadway in a patriotic flag-waving show called *Over The Top*. The show was made up of music and sketches. The music was by Sigmund Romberg, the sketches were written by Harold Atteridge. The leads were played by Justine Johnstone and Mary Eaton. For the first time New Yorkers were able to appraise the talents of Fred and Adele and they liked what they saw. Wrote the critic in *The New York Globe*: 'One of the prettiest features of the show is the dancing

Fred and Adele – elegance personified – at the height of their Broadway fame in the 1920s.

11

Fred and Adele in For Goodness Sake, *the 1922 Broadway show in which they scored their first major hit and in which they made an even bigger impression in London where the show was renamed* Stop Flirting.

of the two Astaires. The girl, a light, spritelike little creature, has really an exquisite floating style in her caperings, while the young man combines eccentric agility with humour.'

Once they had established themselves in *Over The Top*, Fred and Adele never looked back. The show triggered off a kind of chain reaction which resulted in the pair's appearances in a succession of Broadway musicals, each of which enhanced their popularity.

It took six years for them to enjoy a hit all their own but when it came the show made their names on both sides of the Atlantic. Its American title was *For Goodness Sake* (1922). Noel Coward liked what he saw and persuaded them to take the show to London where it was retitled *Stop Flirting* (1923). And in London Fred and Adele enjoyed an even bigger triumph. In New York their show had run for 103 performances. In London it ran for over 400.

Fred and Adele had five songs in *Stop Flirting* with 'Oh Gee, Oh Gosh, Oh Golly, I Love You' stopping the show every night in the middle of the second act. After the first night the pair were toasted by the British show business royalty at

Claridges Hotel although they experienced some trouble getting to the hotel from the Shaftesbury Theatre. 'When we left the stage door, the gallery first-nighters were there *en masse*, some standing on top of our car, some on the hood, all over the place,' wrote Fred later in his autobiography *Steps In Time*.

In London Fred and Adele were embraced by both the aristocracy and royalty and quickly came to epitomise elegance and style. Everyone was taken with their sophistication and charm and they quickly and easily became part of the society scene.

One of their favourite haunts was the famous Savoy Grill where they could often be seen at supper time.

In New York their success continued with a series of shows that ranged from *Lady Be Good* (1924) and *Funny Face* (1927) to *The Band Wagon* (1931). Among the songs they introduced together on Broadway were 'Fascinating Rhythm', 'Swiss Miss' and 'I'd Rather Charleston' in *Lady Be Good*, 'The Babbitt And The Bromide', 'Funny Face' and 'Let's Kiss And Make Up' in *Funny Face*, and 'Hoops', 'Sweet Music' and 'White Heat' in *The*

A cartoonist's view of Fred and Adele in the 1924 George and Ira Gershwin musical Lady Be Good*!*

Band Wagon. The romantic ballads from these shows were not part of Fred's repertoire and such numbers as 'The Man I Love' (*Lady Be Good*), and 'He Loves And She Loves' and 'S'Wonderful' (*Funny Face*) were generally performed by Adele with the show's other male lead.

The sad thing is that there exists no film of Fred and Adele dancing together. All that is left from that golden period of the 1920s are a few photographs, some posters, the acclaim of the critics and – memories. Those who can still recall Adele as a dancer remember her as a young woman with long slim legs, a flashing smile and bold dark eyes. On stage she often wore daffodil dresses and face-framing hats. She had what has been described as a cooey soprano voice. It was *her* style that shaped the team of Fred and Adele, there was no doubt about that.

Fred, of course, was now set on becoming a supreme dancer himself. His sister had set the

Right: *As they appeared in the 'Swiss Miss' number in* Lady Be Good *which ran for 330 performances at New York's Liberty Theatre and a further 326 at the Empire Theatre in London two years later.*

Opposite: *George and Ira Gershwin's 1927 Broadway hit* Funny Face *which premiered at New York's Alvin Theatre on 22 November 1927. The songs included 'My One And Only', 'He Loves And She Loves' and 'S'Wonderful'. Thirty years later it was filmed with a different story line and co-starred Fred and Audrey Hepburn.*

'S WONDERFUL

ALEX A. AARONS AND VINTON FREEDLEY
PRESENT
FRED AND ADELE ASTAIRE
IN THE
NEW MUSICAL COMEDY

Funny Face

MUSIC BY
GEORGE GERSHWIN

BOOK BY
FRED THOMPSON
AND
ROBERT BENCHLEY

LYRICS BY
IRA GERSHWIN

DANCES AND ENSEMBLES BY
ROBERT CONNOLLY
BOOK DIRECTED BY
EDGAR MacGREGOR

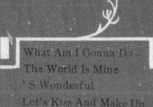

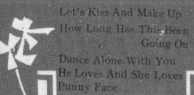

MADE IN U.S.A.

NEW WORLD MUSIC
CORPORATION
HARMS
NEW YORK

GOOD .. they've got to be good!

THEY'RE MILDER, FRED

TASTE BETTER, TOO!

Fred and Adele Astaire in Broadway's musical hit, "The Band Wagon"

Darn good—you'll say!

Everybody wants a mild cigarette. And when you find one that is milder and *tastes better* too—you've got a smoke! Chesterfields are so much milder that you can smoke as many as you like. Mild, ripe, sweet-tasting tobaccos — the best that money can buy. That's what it takes to make a cigarette as good as Chesterfield. And the *purest* cigarette paper!

Every Chesterfield is well-filled. Burns evenly. Smokes cool and comfortable. *They Satisfy* sums it all up!

EVERYBODY'S GETTING ON "THE BAND WAGON"

example and he was determined to follow it. Things hadn't been easy for him. Since childhood he had lived in Adele's shadow and 'gone along with dancing just for the hell of it'. He had realised early on that people considered Adele to be the superior partner and he had accepted it with good grace. He adored Adele and did everything he could to make her the perfect partner. If he bore any resentment or felt jealous at any time he never showed it other than perhaps subjectively when on stage. A reviewer in the *Boston Record* wrote about one of their late vaudeville routines in 1916: 'Fred and Adele Astaire give a fine exhibition of whirlwind dancing although it could be wished that the young man give up some of the blasé air which he constantly carries with him. He is too young for it and it deceives no-one.'

It may well have been that Fred appeared blasé because he had become bored with playing second fiddle to Adele and was too polite to do anything about it. No matter, although his New York shows with Adele made her the toast of the town they also allowed him more than his fair share of the limelight. And as the shows continued he began to find that he too had obtained a whole army of fans. He began to develop his dancing and assert his independence in a series of solo turns many of which had already achieved a wizard-like perfection. Gradually too, the lazy, elegant style he was to make all his own on screen was beginning to emerge. At least once every night on Broadway he would bring the audience to its feet in spontaneous applause.

Until 1932 Fred had never starred with anyone

Above: *The 'I Love Louisa' number from the 1931 Broadway musical of Arthur Schwartz and Howard Dietz*, The Band Wagon. *From left to right: Tilly Losch, Fred, Adele, Frank Morgan and Helen Broderick.*

Opposite: *Smoking doesn't hinder your dancing! At least it didn't in 1931 according to this public endorsement by Fred and Adele.*

17

other than Adele although because of the exigencies of casting he was able on occasion to partner Marilyn Miller and Tilly Losch. But it was always Adele who had been his leading lady. The thought that one day he might well have to carry on without her, or she without him, crossed his mind several times during the 1920s. As it turned out it was Fred who had to do without Adele. She met and fell in love with Lord Charles Cavendish and married into the English aristocracy in 1932. Her last show was *The Band Wagon* which premiered at New York's New Amsterdam Theatre in 1931 and ran for 260 performances. Adele never danced on stage again.

For Fred it was both a sad and a happy time. The sadness was obviously brought about because he realised it was unlikely that he would ever dance with Adele again. The happiness began when he met a pretty 23-year-old socialite named Phyllis Potter. She was much sought after in New York society and was in the process of getting a divorce from her husband by whom she had a three-year-old son. Fred first met her at the race-track but wasn't officially introduced until one Sunday afternoon at the luxury home of Mrs Graham Vanderbilt. For Fred it was an instant attraction. For Phyllis, however, who was not acquainted with the theatre world, Fred took a bit

of getting used to. She certainly found him attractive but he had to pursue her. He even had to persuade her to see him perform in *The Band Wagon*. His charm and powers of persuasion eventually won the day and she at last succumbed, not only to paying a visit to the New Amsterdam Theatre but also to marrying him in July 1933. In Fred's own words 'Phyllis had so many beaux I had to mow them down, one at a time.' The marriage was to last for over 20 years. It was to prove an idyllic relationship.

Within the space of just 14 months (May 1932 to July 1933) Fred had thus lost a lifelong dancing partner and gained a wife. And if that wasn't enough, right in the middle of things (29 November 1932) he gained another dancing partner in the form of Claire Luce who shared the lead with him in the Cole Porter musical *The Gay Divorce*.

Claire Luce was no Adele but she was a very, very competent dancer. And she also allowed Fred to enjoy, for the first time on stage, the pleasures of participating in a romantic dance routine. With Adele, Fred's numbers had been based on comedy. In the memorable 'Night And Day' number, danced seductively by Fred and Claire, Fred's stage persona took on a new dimension. Not that the show received good notices. At best they were

Opposite: *Fred and Adele in the comedy 'Hoops' number from* The Band Wagon.

Below: *The marriage of Lord Charles Cavendish and Adele Astaire. Left to right – the adults: Mrs Astaire, the bride, the bridegroom, Mr Henry Hunloke (best man) and the Duke of Devonshire. The children: Peter, Michael and Judith Baillie and Elizabeth and Anne Cavendish.*

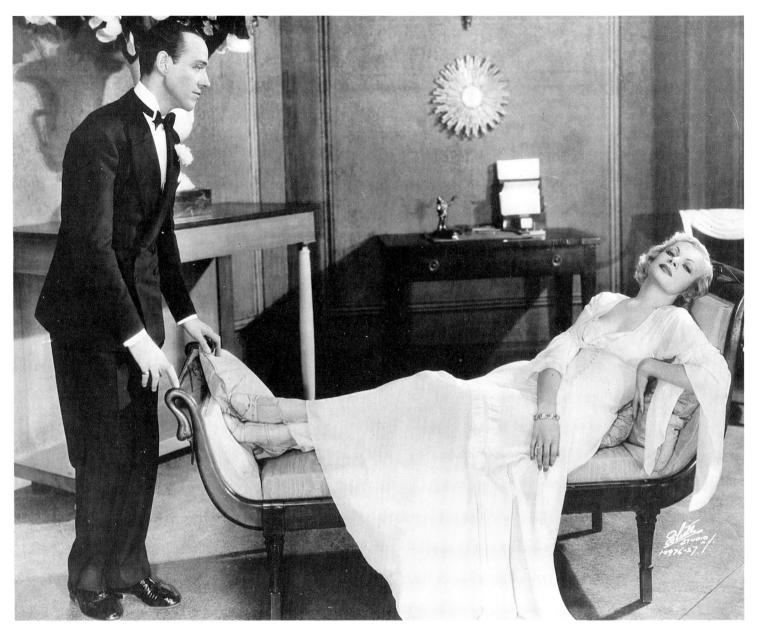

Above: *Fred with his first romantic dancing partner, Claire Luce, who shared the evergreen 'Night and Day' number with him on the Broadway and London stage.*

Opposite: *Ready for Hollywood! Fred and his wife Phyllis arrive in the movie capital in July 1933.*

lukewarm. Some might say, tepid. The press notice most often quoted is the one which read: 'Fred Astaire stops every now and then to look off stage towards the wings as if he were hoping his titled sister, Adele, would come out and rescue him.'

In an effort to keep the show ticking over the management of the theatre threw the balcony open to cut-rate tickets. The huge success of 'Night And Day' which became a best-selling song also helped things. But what Fred was most hoping for didn't happen, at least not when he expected it to. With Adele now retired he had the movies firmly in mind. He also entertained the hope that someone from one of the major studios would see *The Gay Divorcee*, buy the screen rights and take him along as part of the package. It would be a breakthrough into the movies and in a starring role. But although Warners had been approached by director Mervyn LeRoy who had seen the show early in its run, they turned it down. Jack Warner's comment was: 'Who am I going to put in it, Cagney?'

Instead Fred was offered a supporting role in a movie that might or might not be a success and that

was being produced by one of Hollywood's less glamorous studios, RKO. And it was with that film in mind that he made the long, 26-hour plane journey to Los Angeles in the summer of 1933.

Phyllis was by his side which was a comfort, but nagging him was one terrible doubt. Five years earlier in 1928 he had made a screen test at Paramount when the studio had been thinking of bringing *Funny Face* to the screen. Adele had also been tested and had passed with flying colours. Not Fred. The supposed verdict on his test read: 'Can't act. Can't sing. Balding. Can dance a little.'

Whether anyone ever said or wrote those famous words is doubtful. No-one ever claimed authorship and the comment belongs more with Hollywood mythology than Hollywood fact. But the fact remained, Fred had been turned down once, no matter what the reason. And he knew that Hollywood was already littered with screen careers that were over before they ever got started. It was small wonder that he was viewing the future with anxiety when he and Phyllis landed at Burbank in 1933.

MC-31799

TOP HAT, WHITE TIE AND TAILS

Fred with his first ever screen dancing partner, Joan Crawford, in the 'Heigh-Ho, The Gang's All Here' number from Dancing Lady *(MGM, 1933).*

In many ways it was a good thing that Fred's famous screen test turned out the way it did. If things had gone the other way and Fred had been immediately accepted as star material he would have started his film career somewhere around 1928/1929. And that would have been a bad time to start for although *The Broadway Melody* won an Academy Award as best film of the year, thus indicating that musicals had achieved respectability, the Oscar was misleading. Musicals were not on the way up. They were on the way down. And Fred's career, had he appeared in *Funny Face*, might have gone down with them.

In fact, shortly after the release of MGM's *The Broadway Melody*, the public began to tire very quickly of screen musical entertainments. The novelty of watching stars sing and dance had worn off, as had the novelty of talking pictures. Most of the musicals were no more than revues anyhow and the general consensus was that once you'd seen one you'd seen them all. And so it proved. In the early 1930s musicals began to disappear from the production schedules at an alarming rate. By 1932 they were, to all intents and purposes, dead. The public welcomed comedies, westerns, soap operas, even the new horror films from Universal. But they turned their backs on the musical.

It was only due to the efforts of Darryl F. Zanuck, who had made something of a name for himself at Warners, first as a writer, then as a dynamic young producer, that musicals eventually managed to get off the ground again. He persuaded his boss, Jack L. Warner, to have one last crack at musicals. He brought in Busby Berkeley as dance director/choreographer and pepped up what was the corniest of stories (a young unknown becomes the star of a Broadway show when the leading lady has to cry off because of a twisted ankle) with a number of lavish and brilliantly staged dancing sequences and tuneful Harry Warren/Al Dubin songs. He called the film *42nd Street*. It made money and it made the headlines. With just the one film Zanuck brought the musical back to prominence. And it stayed back.

The success of *42nd Street* meant, of course, that the other Hollywood studios also began to have second thoughts about the musical. MGM started in on the genre once more as did Paramount. And

so too did the rather less fashionable studio of RKO. And that's where Fred entered into the scheme of things for it was at RKO, a small-scale outfit looked down on in Hollywood and rather unkindly referred to as 'the studio of falling stars', that he was scheduled to make his first screen appearance.

It didn't quite turn out that way for while he was preparing for the RKO movie, titled *Flying Down To Rio*, he received an offer from MGM to feature in a guest spot in their Joan Crawford/Clark Gable picture *Dancing Lady* (1933).

It wasn't much of a spot. In fact, Fred was on screen for just 4 minutes and 50 seconds. But it did at least give him the chance to demonstrate what he could do. Dressed in the attire that was to make him a household name across the world – top hat, white tie and tails – he danced twice in the picture. His partner on both occasions was Miss Crawford, not the most elegant of hoofers. Their numbers were 'Heigh Ho, The Gang's All Here' and 'Let's Go Bavarian', both composed by Burton Lane and Harold Adamson. Fred commented that as far as he was concerned he looked like a knife. He was unimpressed. Phyllis naturally enough thought he looked charming, which at least went some way to helping Fred's confidence as he settled down to prepare for his first real test in *Flying Down To Rio*.

He had originally expected that his partner in the movie was to be an actress named Dorothy Jordan. But she married executive producer Merian C. Cooper and quickly dropped out of the running.

Her place was taken by a young red-headed 21-year-old named Ginger Rogers. Ginger had featured as one of the supporting players in the historic *42nd Street* at Warners. She'd played a chorus girl called 'Anytime Annie'. She not only made with the wisecracks but was also on the receiving end: 'The only time Anytime Annie said no, she didn't hear the question!' On top of that she sang her way through a few choruses of 'Shuffle Off To Buffalo' with Una Merkel. It was a smallish part as was her role in Warner's subsequent *Gold Diggers Of 1933*.

One of the reasons Ginger decided on a move from Warners was that it was fast filling up with musical talent and she felt it might be tough

The trade advertisement
for Fred and Ginger's
first film together Flying
Down to Rio (RKO,
1933).

Above: *Fred and Ginger size each other up – and not for the last time – in* Flying Down To Rio *(RKO, 1933).*

Opposite: *'The Carioca' – Fred and Ginger dance together for the first time on screen in* Flying Down To Rio *(RKO, 1933).*

breaking into the big time at the studio. Another was that she didn't really want to become typed as a musical star. She wanted to prove herself both as a comedienne and dramatic actress. And she felt that she would stand a better chance by moving to another studio.

Harry Cohn, the crude-talking boss of Columbia, almost snapped her up but took so long in making up his mind that in the end Ginger signed a seven-year contract at RKO. She knew it wasn't the best studio in town. Not by a long way. But it was a friendly place and it might just give her the chance to break away from the musical mould. Little did she realise what signing that contract would eventually come to mean.

At first, it meant very little. When she was told that she was to dance with Fred in *Flying Down to Rio*, she simply took it in her stride. 'Oh well,' she said to Fred, 'It's just another musical, let's do it and have some fun.' To her, of course, it *was* just another musical. Even though she was only 21 she was already the veteran of some 20 films, made in just 4 years. For Fred it was *the* musical. He was billed only fifth (to Ginger's fourth) but he knew just how much depended on the picture.

The two top stars in *Flying Down To Rio* were Dolores Del Rio and Gene Raymond. The story (such as it was) was about a girl who is torn between her Brazilian fiancé and an American orchestra leader who stages a dramatic airborne opening for her father's new resort hotel in Rio. Not surprisingly the aviator, assisted by dancer Fred and vocalist Ginger, wins the girl. The film closes spectacularly with an aerial circus with dancing girls peforming on the wings of planes as they fly (courtesy of trick photography) over Rio Bay.

The RKO publicists had promised a film 'Where lovely Brazilian ladies will catch your eye/ by the light of a million stars in the evening sky'. What they didn't promise (indeed how could they, they didn't know!) was that it wouldn't be the Brazilian lovelies or the stars in the sky that would catch the eye, but Fred and Ginger.

As soon as they came together on the dance floor something magical happened. It was one of those indefinable things, like star quality, that even today defies explanation. The combination of a skinny, plain-faced little fellow with the nimblest toes in the business and a pretty, down-to-earth girl

Between takes! Fred and Ginger and the huge supporting cast plan 'The Carioca' in Flying Down To Rio *(RKO, 1933).*

somehow blended perfectly. In many ways it shouldn't have done for they were complete opposites but possibly because their personalities *were* so different they produced a chemistry that worked beautifully and caught the imagination of the public.

And not only did they please the public. The critics were quite satisfied as well. They particularly singled out 'The Carioca' as well they might for the number (composed by Vincent Youmans with lyrics by Edward Eliscu and Gus Kahn) ran for over four minutes on screen. Hollywood mythology has it that it took over a hundred hours to rehearse and, looking at it today, one can well believe it.

'The Carioca' made the world realise that in 1933 something very special had occurred as far as films were concerned. Fred and Ginger had arrived. As they danced together on top of seven white pianos, surrounded by a host of swaying chorus girls, they danced their way not only into the history books but also into the profit columns of the RKO accounts' ledgers, a most welcome achievement as far as the studio was concerned for they were not used to such financial success.

As the picture enjoyed a record-breaking run at

New York's Radio City Music Hall the studio bosses realised that they had stumbled on to the perfect musical combination.

Oddly enough, Fred and Ginger were apart more than they were together in *Flying Down To Rio*. The song 'Music Makes Me' was sung by Ginger and later reprised by Fred as a tap solo; 'Flying Down To Rio' was sung by Fred (together with chorus); and 'Orchids In The Moonlight' was danced by Fred and Dolores Del Rio. Only in the rhythmic, pulsating rhumba-like dance 'The Carioca' did they come together. But the one dance was enough.

For Fred, however, the success of the picture was to remain an unknown quantity for some time. In fact, once he had finished shooting, he was unsure of the effect he would have on screen audiences. He had serious doubts that he was star material. He believed in himself as a dancer. He had no doubts on that score. And he thought that he might just get by as a light comedian. But he never thought he would make it above character actor status. He said later: 'I came out to Hollywood because I was anxious to see what the movie thing was all about and I didn't think perhaps that I would make it. I was a weird-looking character

anyway and I never liked the way I photographed particularly. I don't think many people did either. However, that didn't matter after they'd got used to you. As long as you had what they felt was some sort of personality that worked, that's what counted.'

Fred and Ginger weren't the only ones who got together on *Flying Down To Rio*. Choreographer Hermes Pan who was assigned as assistant to dance director David Gould also encountered Fred for the first time. They met up when Fred was rehearsing one of his routines. Pan had been sent up to Fred to see if he could help in any way. Aware of Fred's reputation for perfectionism Pan was tentative about suggesting anything and was quite prepared to stand and watch. But when Fred admitted that he'd hit a sticky patch and was unsure which way to go next Pan came up with a suggestion that Fred liked and eventually used in the film. Pan always remembers that first meeting. It gave him confidence and helped him on his way in films. From that moment, a life-long friendship, one that stretched from *Flying Down To Rio* to *Finian's Rainbow*, was forged.

Fred had been signed by RKO for the one picture only so that when he embarked with Phyllis for London for the British stage version of *The Gay Divorce* (1933), he was not under any kind of long term contract. The film was still in the editing stages and had not been previewed so no-one quite knew what they had in the can. Fred certainly had his doubts about his future in films. As he was making his goodbyes to the various people he had got to know on the lot he told Ginger that he thought dancing on screen had something of a limited future. He also mentioned to the RKO top brass that it might be better if they cut out his numbers altogether and turn the film into a comedy without music. Failing that, he told them, he was quite prepared to shoot all his numbers again.

RKO wisely ignored his doubts and went on editing *Flying Down To Rio*, gradually becoming aware that they might have a big hit on their hands.

Meanwhile, Fred headed for England and a return to the stage. Because of his workload he had been unable to enjoy a honeymoon with Phyllis so the trip was treated as one. The honeymoon may have been fun but the rest of the stay proved something of a nightmare.

The thing that upset Fred most was that his sister gave birth prematurely to a baby girl who

Fred sings the title song from Flying Down to Rio *(RKO, 1933).*

FRED ASTAIRE
GINGER ROGERS

THE KING
AND QUEEN
of "CARIOCA" in

THE GAY DIVORCEE

WITH

ALICE BRADY
Edward Everett HORTON

DIRECTED BY MARK SANDRICH
A PANDRO S. BERMAN PRODUCTION

RKO Radio PICTURES

died almost immediately. Adele, desperately upset, was heart-broken and remained ill for weeks. Both Fred and Phyllis did what they could to console her but it was a bad time for all of them. Adele's illness meant that she had to miss Fred's opening night. In view of what occurred on that opening night it's more than likely that Fred's partner, once again Claire Luce, wished she had missed it too. As she and Fred went into one of their numbers – one in which they had to dance over the furniture – she tripped and both she and Fred went sprawling.

Somehow Claire got through the show even though she had damaged her hip and was in some pain for the rest of the performance. She also carried on in the show for the rest of the run but that fall on stage eventually resulted in a lengthy stay in hospital and the end of her dancing career.

All things considered the English trip had not turned out to be the happiest of occasions even though the show which opened at the Palace ran for over a hundred performances. Adele did eventually go to see it and remarked that she was amazed at Fred's sex appeal on stage. It was of course the first time she had seen him from front

row stalls and not actually danced with him in a musical play.

All the time he was in London Fred kept wondering what was happening back in Hollywood. Despite his personal doubts about his abilities on screen he was still anxious to try to make it in the movies. He sensed that that was where his future lay, so in retrospect at least, the success of *Flying Down To Rio* became important to him.

As the New York opening of the film drew nearer he became so nervous that he refused to open any cables from the States in case they spelt what he secretly feared most – disaster! His fears proved groundless. When a cable from RKO did arrive it assured him that both he and Ginger – and the film – were a smash.

The cable came from a young producer named Pandro S. Berman and also offered Fred a seven-year contract with the studio. What is more, Berman suggested that Fred's next film project might be *The Gay Divorce*, the very musical play with which Fred had hoped he would start his film career.

Fred was both relieved and delighted. He said

Above: *The famous trademark for RKO, the studio that launched the Astaire/Rogers partnership during the 1930s and because of the pair's success was saved from bankruptcy.*

Opposite: *'The king and queen of Carioca' get their names above the title for the first time in the 1934 hit* The Gay Divorcee *(RKO).*

yes to both proposals and when the London run of *The Gay Divorce* came to an end headed back to Hollywood and RKO with Phyllis.

Lou Brock had been his producer on *Flying Down To Rio*. He might also have been the producer of *The Gay Divorcee* (1934) (the title was changed because the word divorce was thought 'uncommercial' although the original title was retained in Britain) had he had the foresight to see that the show would make an excellent musical on screen. Berman offered him the chance but Brock's answer was that he could blow a better script out of his nose. Berman who was then both a producer and the head of production at RKO decided to make it instead.

There was mention initially that Diana Wynyard might possibly be Fred's partner in *The Gay Divorcee*. Berman ignored the rumours. He knew that the public had acclaimed *Flying Down To Rio* for one reason only – Fred and Ginger. They had sensed something that Katherine Hepburn was to put very succinctly in just one sentence: 'He gives her class, she gives him sex.'

Berman had quite a bit of persuading to do, however. Neither Fred nor Ginger was over-ecstatic about the prospect of working with the other again. There was no animosity and they didn't dislike working together. It was just that their aims were different. Ginger still clung to her ambitions of making it in films other than musicals and Fred, for his part, would have preferred to have worked solo. Berman later recalled: 'He never got over the feeling that he was being forced into being a member of a team, which was the last thing in the world that he wanted.'

Above: *Fred beckons, Ginger stays aloof. An early encounter in* The Gay Divorcee *(RKO, 1934).*

Right: *Fred persists and Ginger begins to melt.* The Gay Divorcee *(RKO, 1934).*

Opposite: *Fred and Ginger make movie history with 'The Continental', the first song to be awarded an Oscar as best of the year. The film,* The Gay Divorcee *was released by RKO in 1934.*

Nonetheless, the early 1930s was the time when the Hollywood studios had their stars firmly under long-term contracts. Stars did what they were told, otherwise it meant suspension. So Fred agreed to have Ginger as his partner and Ginger went ahead and danced with Fred. And at least she had the consolation of knowing that not every film she was to make at RKO would be a musical. For every film with Fred there would be two, sometimes three, others that would develop her talents in other directions and allow her to work with such film makers as George Stevens and Gregory La Cava.

As for Fred, well, his status was assured even before he appeared in a single scene in *The Gay Divorcee*. RKO thought so highly of him as an investment that they insured his legs for £200,000!

They also hired Hermes Pan once more to work as assistant to dance director Dave Gould. He, more than anyone else, quickly came to realise that although the plots of the Astaire/Rogers films were essentially lightweight affairs – *The Gay Divorcee* was about dancer Fred being mistaken for the professional co-respondent of divorce-seeking Ginger – the amount of work put into their filming was anything but insubstantial.

This was especially true when it came to filming the picture's big number, 'The Continental', a song that had been added to the show's original score (only 'Night And Day' remained) by composers Con Conrad and Harry Revel and lyricists Herb Magidson and Mack Gordon.

The song had been released by RKO before the picture's premiere and was being played by dance bands all over the country. On screen its theme was repeated over and over again for something like 17 minutes which made it the longest number ever to be staged around one song on screen. Remembered Pan: 'All I can recall about "The Continental" in *The Gay Divorcee* was that it was blood, sweat and tears. I had this charge of 32 girls and 32 boys and I worked out the steps. We used to work them from 10 in the morning till 10 at night. And no overtime. It was really a tough job.' Fred also worked overtime as he always did both in his numbers with Ginger and on his solos. These included the dazzling 'Don't Let It Bother You' in which the proprietor of a Paris night club forces Fred to dance for his supper, and 'Needle In A Haystack' in which Fred dresses to the music, discarding a dressing-gown and donning a tie and

JEROME KERN'S QUEEN OF MUSICAL ROMANCES ROBERTA

Above: Roberta *in which Fred and Ginger shared top billing with Irene Dunne.*

Opposite: *RKO's three-tier set for* Roberta. *In 1935 the studio announced that the camera was on the largest camera crane in the world. Randolph Scott, director William Seiter and Fred Astaire can be glimpsed in the centre of the third floor.*

jacket, before leaping nimbly across the furniture and grabbing an umbrella and sailing forth into the street.

It's difficult to believe that, apart from the climactic 'The Continental' only 10 of *The Gay Divorcee*'s 107 minutes are taken up with Fred dancing alone or with Ginger. The rest is just so much amiable nonsense helped along by such stalwarts as Edward Everett Horton (dense attorney), Eric Blore (waiter) and Erik Rhodes as the real co-respondent. But it says much for the grace and style of the two dancers that those 10 minutes stay in the memory long after the other sections of the film have faded from the mind.

To the casual observer the Fred Astaire/Ginger Rogers films of the 1930s now creak with age. Yet as soon as the comedy passages come to an end and the 'She loves me/Oh, no I don't/Oh yes you do' bit is got out of the way, disbelief is suspended. As soon as the music starts the age of the film is forgotten. The superb 'Night And Day' number with Ginger in a long white dress and Fred in immaculate evening attire is a perfect example. The number has been described as 'a seduction in dance'. The description is close. Dancing (or it seems at times, gliding) to the haunting and

beautiful melody, Fred and Ginger turn the sequence into one of the 1930s' most memorable cinematic moments.

The Astaire/Rogers films may seem simplistic these days, but it should be remembered that in the 1930s that's exactly what the audiences wanted. They knew what was coming before they'd even paid for their tickets. And they didn't mind. They paid to relax with the corn of the stories and the sumptuous elegance of the music. And when the dance numbers arrived they would often break out in spontaneous applause. It was when they realised that simple fact that RKO knew they couldn't miss.

Also, the Astaire/Rogers films were not just another successful series of musical films as is sometimes implied in the history books. They were different. There were no other films of a similar kind being produced at other studios. At Warners huge choruses of leggy girls expanded then contracted then expanded again into Busby Berkeley's fantastic geometric shapes, but there were no two dancers that held single stage for an entire film.

MGM and Paramount were other studios which found it impossible to compete. They had singing teams such as Maurice Chevalier and Jeanette MacDonald, and later Nelson Eddy and Mac-

Right: *Fred and Ginger – still not sure of each other – pictured in* Roberta *(RKO, 1935).*

Below: *'I Won't Dance!' Fred and Ginger in* Roberta *(RKO, 1935).*

Donald. But no dancing teams. Fred had the field to himself and he made the most of it. He was never happier than when he was working alone, when he could invent, re-do, invent a new step, re-do it over again and again and again. Overtime meant nothing to him. Overtime meant pleasure.

Ginger would come in on the numbers later, after he had perfected them as much as he could. During rehearsals, Hermes Pan worked with him and stood in for Ginger. Pandro Berman remembers how they worked it out: 'Fred was a tremendous perfectionist and we took a long time to rehearse the numbers. But it wasn't costly because Fred would go to a little stage somewhere with his associate choreographer Hermes Pan. Then, when they had everything worked out – Hermes playing the role of Ginger during the rehearsal period – we'd finally bring in Ginger and teach her what was required. Then we'd make the picture. During the shooting we'd film the smaller numbers as we came to them but we'd wait till the end to make the big splashy numbers. They were filmed after the picture was finished and all the other actors had ended their stints.'

Pandro Berman was associated with the Astaire/Rogers pictures throughout the 1930s. He always ensured that all of them were given the best production the studio could afford. Art directors Van Nest Polglase and Carroll Clark were the two men chiefly responsible for the look of the movies

for it was they who designed the sumptuous black and white sets of hotel rooms with elegant drapes and balconies and dance floors with shining white marble stairways. Without them and the camerawork of David Abel and the gowns of Bernard Newman the films would have been only half as good as they were.

It wasn't only Fred's twinkling feet and Ginger's vivacious personality that made the films such a treat for the public. It was also Fred's voice. Some people have commented that he could only just carry a tune. Not so. He was for many years one of the best singers of songs in the business. And if there's any query on that score one has only to look down the list of composers and lyricists who queued up to work for him – Cole Porter, Jerome Kern, Irving Berling (many, many times), Con Conrad and Herb Magidson – to name but a few.

And in 1934 Conrad and Magidson were well rewarded for their efforts. 'The Continental' became the first song to win an Oscar as the best of the year. Before 1934 there had been no such category at the awards ceremony. It was only fitting that a song from an Astaire/Rogers movie should emerge as the first winner.

The Gay Divorcee was also nominated as one of the best pictures of the year. Its critical notices were superb. Andre Sennwald wrote in *The New York Times*: 'Last season it was "The Carioca" which persuaded the foolhardy to bash their heads together. Now the athletic RKO-Radio's strategists have created "The Continental", an equally strenuous routine in which you confide your secret dreams to your partner under the protective camouflage of the music. . . . Both as a romantic comedian and as a lyric dancer, Mr Astaire is an urbane delight, and Miss Rogers keeps pace with him even in his rhythmic flights over the furniture.'

Pandro Berman, not altogether surprisingly, remembers the Astaire/Rogers musicals as much for their profits as their artistic success. 'They were tremendous moneymakers for us in the sense that it was the worst time in the history of the film business. No pictures were doing the kind of business they came to do later in the 1930s. For example, $1 million gross was considered tremendous by MGM, the biggest company in the business with the biggest stars. These pictures starred people like Garbo, Joan Crawford, Gable,

Fred and Ginger glide elegantly through Jerome Kern's 'Smoke Gets In Your Eyes' in Roberta *(RKO, 1935).*

Wallace Beery, Marie Dressler, people like that. If they did $1 million that was tremendous. Well, we did $3 million with the first Fred Astaire movie and we did the same with the next 5 or 6. I guess that's the equivalent of maybe $40 million today, in terms of today's costs and today's market. The pictures pulled us out of bankruptcy. They made us go into profit. And that was fabulous.'

After *The Gay Divorcee* Fred managed to get a little time off. But not much. He spent some time playing golf with Phyllis, who by now had settled nicely into a quiet Hollywood routine, and also embarked with her on the occasional deep-sea fishing trip. But in those days there wasn't too much time for leisure. No sooner had one Astaire/ Rogers movie been released than another was being rehearsed and yet another was being planned for the following year. A Hollywood director once described the studios as huge sausage factories. And he wasn't too wide of the mark. RKO was no different from all the rest.

The next picture Berman had lined up for Fred and Ginger was *Roberta* (1935) which he had purchased at the same time he had bought *The Gay Divorcee*. He bought it for $65,000, outbidding both Paramount and MGM. This time he added two new ingredients – Irene Dunne who took top billing and Randolph Scott. And it was a question of having to for the story of *Roberta* revolved not around two characters but four.

Its rather ridiculous double romance plot centred on an all-American football hero (Scott) who inherits his aunt's chic Parisian fashion house and wins the hand of a Russian princess turned dress designer (Dunne) along the way. Helping

Above: *'I'll Be Hard To Handle' – Fred and Ginger at the top of their form as they dance together in an informal session on a dance floor in* Roberta *(RKO, 1935).*

Right: *Fred and his troupe of Wabash Indians in the 'Organ Number' in* Roberta *(RKO, 1935).*

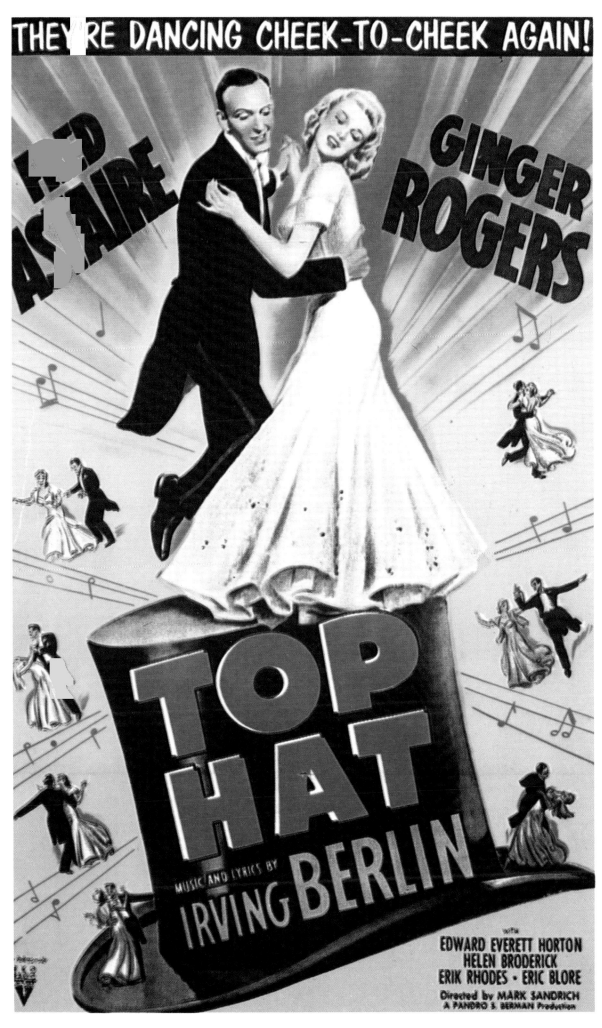

THEY'RE DANCING CHEEK-TO-CHEEK AGAIN!

FRED ASTAIRE

GINGER ROGERS

TOP HAT

MUSIC AND LYRICS BY IRVING BERLIN

with
EDWARD EVERETT HORTON
HELEN BRODERICK
ERIK RHODES · ERIC BLORE
Directed by MARK SANDRICH
A PANDRO S. BERMAN Production

Top Hat *(RKO, 1935)!*
Arguably the best of all the Astaire/Rogers musicals of the 1930s and winner of four Oscar nominations including a mention as best picture of the year.

Right: *Fred and Ginger relaxing with director Mark Sandrich (left) and composer Irving Berlin (right) outside the RKO sound stages during the filming of* Top Hat *(RKO, 1935).*

Below: *Practice . . . practice . . . practice. Fred and Ginger rehearse one of the Irving Berlin numbers in* Top Hat. *Composer Berlin, seated at the piano, looks on.*

things out are Fred as Scott's musical buddy and Ginger as a nightclub singer posing as a Polish countess. Between them they manage to turn the fashion house into a going concern, with a gigantic fashion show as the climax.

Much of the plot was tedious. So too was Ginger's deliberately and eventually boringly phoney accent. But the film burst into life during its musical sequences, not least in the 'Lovely To Look At' number, sung first by Irene Dunne, and the electrifying 'I Won't Dance' sung first by Ginger and then danced solo by Fred.

Fred and Ginger also got their teeth (and feet) into the 'I'll Be Hard To Handle' number, the first of their 'rivalry' routines in which one tries to outdo the other on the dance floor, and the poignant and tender 'Smoke Gets In Your Eyes'.

Fred always rated the latter song as one of the best numbers he had ever danced to. He also knew that audiences entering the cinemas would be expecting a big dance number to the song. And

neither he nor Ginger disappointed them even though during rehearsals Ginger asked Fred if he didn't think it was a bit on the slow side. To which Fred replied: 'Yes, but that's the way I think it should be.' Ginger, used to being overruled in such matters, simply shrugged and said, 'I guess you're right, Fred'. And as usual he was.

Roberta was the first film on which Hermes Pan got a solo credit as dance director even though, to all intents and purposes, he was doing exactly the same job he had been doing on the previous two pictures he'd made with Fred and Ginger. It was during the filming of the picture that Fred became more and more interested in the film medium. He was always striving for perfection in his dance numbers and rarely, if ever, would be satisfied with his performance. When watching himself on screen he would always comment, 'He isn't doing that right'. Like Judy Garland and Katharine Hepburn he would always use the third person when discussing his screen work.

While working on *Roberta* he spent hours in the cutting rooms, making sure that the sound was right and synchronised with his taps. Most people wouldn't have bothered with such details and would have left it to the technicians to work out. Not Fred. He strove for hours to get what he wanted. Even before shooting began on *Roberta* he spent nine weeks solidly rehearsing his numbers. And weeks usually included Saturday and Sunday. Sometimes he would work out a routine before the music arrived and on one occasion astonished Jerome Kern by dancing one of the numbers through the composer's house.

Irene Dunne said: 'Fred was known as the number one worrier in Hollywood. He was such a perfectionist about his routines. He was always a pleasure to work with but heaven help anyone who didn't do his job well.'

The RKO publicity department left nothing to chance when promoting *Roberta*. Said the ads: 'Jerome Kern's dazzling stage success . . . ten times as tantalizing on the screen . . . a heartload of romance in Paris at love time . . . a lifetime of

The evening wear is discarded for once as Fred and Ginger share the bandstand number 'Isn't This A Lovely Day' in Top Hat *(RKO, 1935).*

'Cheek to Cheek', one of the loveliest and most elegant of all the Astaire/Rogers numbers but one of the most difficult to film. Top Hat (RKO, 1935).

laughter! . . . a world of joy! . . . a riot of rhythm . . . a screenful of dancing!'

Whether anyone ever actually believed all the ludicrous hyperbole back in the 1930s is difficult to say. Certainly today it sounds amusing and over the top but in those dark days of the depression just about anything seemed believable, even Fred and Ginger in their glamorous make-believe world – a world that most of those making up cinema audiences around the world would never experience in real life.

The critic for *Time* magazine summed up *Roberta* best when he wrote: 'The most pleasant moments in *Roberta* arrive when Fred Astaire and Ginger Rogers turn the story upside down and dance on it. On the three occasions when they allow their feet to speak for them, their sleek and nimble scufflings lift *Roberta* out of the class of ordinary entertainment and make it an intermittent masterpiece. The picture establishes Fred Astaire more firmly than ever as the number one hoofer of the cinema and proves what *The Gay Divorcee* suggested: that Ginger Rogers is a wholly acceptable partner.'

Roberta earned RKO $770,000 in profits and boosted the careers of its two stars still further. The fact that it was released in 1935, the year of release of *Becky Sharp* (the first feature to be shot in the three-colour Technicolor process) has often given rise to the question: Why, in the 1930s, were not some of the Astaire/Rogers musicals shot in colour?

There are several answers. One is that the cost was prohibitive; another that the dazzling black and white sets of Van Nest Polglase and Carroll Clark were attractive enough as they were. A third is that the colour itself was not up to much. Pandro

A sequence from 'Cheek To Cheek' in Top Hat *(RKO, 1935).*

Berman remembers: 'We were not in the position to spend the money and the colour wasn't very good in those days. We had experimented with it a little bit. We had made the last reel or two of *Rio Rita* in colour, back in Bill LeBaron's days, after making most of it in black and white. But colour wasn't all that exciting to us and we didn't feel the need to use it.'

The point is well made, especially when you take into account the cost of the Astaire/Rogers pictures without colour. Says Berman: 'The first picture cost $540,000, the second picture a few dollars more and by the time I finished the nine, only the last picture came close to a million. Most of them were made in the $600,000 category. But they were the days when you could make everything very cheaply because we were going through the worst depression in our history.'

One person Berman did get cheaply was a then very young and very raw Lucille Ball. She had already appeared in movies but *Roberta* was the first film she made for RKO. Berman put her under contract because he was looking for suitable candidates for the film's fashion show. He paid her about $50 a week. Some 22 years later her production company Desilu would purchase the entire RKO studio for the production of television programmes.

The very next Astaire/Rogers movie was one of those that cost around the $600,000 figure. And for many people it remains the best film the two stars ever made together. Nominated for four Academy Awards including best picture, it seemed in 1935 to be just about perfect in every department. The earlier Astaire/Rogers musicals had all had their fair share of faults as did several of those

47

that followed later in the decade but somehow, in *Top Hat*, everything seemed to blend together, the talents of everyone involved were shown off at their very best.

Fred himself certainly liked the movie and said so on several occasions. He has often commented that he regards it as a kind of movie standard that has about it a timeless appeal and that it never seems to age.

One of the reasons why Fred remains so enamoured with the picture is that it was the first of his films for which Irving Berlin wrote the score. Cole Porter and Jerome Kern had already written for him. Now it was Irving Berlin's turn. All in all it was a pretty good trio for someone who just three years before had been worried about whether he had any future in movies.

Berlin was signed by Pandro Berman to write two pictures for Fred. He commented later that he would never have written some of his most successful numbers if he hadn't had Fred Astaire to write for. The same applies to other composers but if Berlin's comment needs justifying one has only to look at and listen to *Top Hat*. There isn't a dud song in it. It's a short score (just five songs — one was dropped, 'Get Thee Behind Me Satan' because it slowed down the plot) but it still ranks with the five best-ever written directly for a movie.

The plot of *Top Hat* is as usual as light as a soufflé. Fred's an American dancer working on the London stage. He falls for socialite Ginger and pursues her to Venice where she thinks he is the husband of her best friend. The misunderstandings multiply but in the end everything is sorted out so that Fred can rescue Ginger from her rebound marriage to dress designer Erik Rhodes.

Berlin's songs punctuate the story at frequent intervals. The 'No Strings' number has Fred doing a wonderful solo and dance above Ginger's hotel room and sprinkling sawdust on the floor so he doesn't wake her; the massive, climactic 'The Piccolino' is built along the same lines as the earlier 'The Carioca' and 'The Continental' numbers; and the charming 'Isn't This A Lovely Day' has Ginger and Fred caught in a storm in Hyde Park and taking shelter in a bandstand. Within the confined setting of the bandstand he begins to court her through dance. She is dressed in riding habit, he in a lounge suit. Hostile to his attentions at first, she eventually melts to his persistence and charm.

The two numbers that were the most trouble to film were 'Cheek To Cheek' and Fred's brilliant solo to the title song.

'Cheek To Cheek', one of the most romantic numbers Fred and Ginger ever performed together, was anything but romantic to film. Fred was in his usual immaculate evening attire, Ginger was in a gown of light turquoise satin, accented with ostrich feathers. And it was the feathers that caused the trouble. Every time the pair took a few steps, feathers would fly off the dress. Sometimes they would fly at the camera, sometimes up Fred's nose or in his eyes. But fly they most certainly did.

Fred cussed the dress no end of times before the number was completed. In the end, so it *was* completed, designer Bernard Newman had each single strand of the dress knotted!

The 'Top Hat' number was the one on which Fred really lost his temper, not with anyone working on the film, but with himself. He had rehearsed it for two months. In it he dances solo with his cane and then, still tapping, machine-guns a male chorus line all dressed in top hat, white tie and tails. The cane acts as the machine-gun!

The big problem as far as the studio prop people were concerned was how many canes to order. They thought that things might not go well the first time so they played safe and ordered a dozen. Even allowing for the fact that there would almost certainly be plenty of retakes, they reckoned that ought to be enough. But just for the heck of it, they ordered 13.

It turned out to be a lucky 13 for it wasn't until he was on cane number 13, having broken the previous 12 over his knee in exasperation, that Fred finally completed the number to his satisfaction. It took him 40 takes to get 'Top Hat' right. And in the end he chose take one.

One of the visitors who came to watch the number being filmed was Warner star James Cagney who by then had earned himself something of a reputation as a hoofer at his studio. He watched in admiration as Fred went through his routine. After the number the two got talking. One day, Fred told Cagney, they would do a number together on screen. The two actors shook on it, vowing that they'd have to get it done before they got too old. They left it too late. The opportunity never arose. Fred and Jimmy Cagney never danced together on screen. If they had, it almost certainly would have been something to behold.

Everyone did their best to make *Top Hat* a witty, engaging and delightful experience: director Mark Sandrich, a regular on the Astaire/Rogers films in the 1930s, Irving Berlin, set designers Van Nest Polglase and Carroll Clark, the usual supporting players, among them Edward Everett Horton, Eric Blore and Erik Rhodes. But in the end, of course it was Fred and Ginger's show. One critic actually mentioned that during the dance in the bandstand he even forgot he was watching a movie.

The film opened in August 1935 at the Radio City Music Hall and smashed all attendance records. It grossed $3,200,000 making it the most lucrative RKO film of the decade. Only MGM's *Mutiny On The Bounty*, voted the year's best at Oscar time, earned more.

For the first time since 1930 the RKO studio made a profit, nearly $700,000. The studio expanded. Three new sound stages, dressing-rooms, scene docks, film vaults and a three-storey office building were added. Most of the expenditure came out of the profits of *Top Hat*!

Fred's rivals in dance –
each one mowed down by
Fred's 'machine-gun'
cane. Top Hat *(RKO,*
1935).

SWING TIME

Opposite: *A bell-
bottomed Fred performing
a tap routine to Irving
Berlin's 'I'd Rather Lead
A Band' in* Follow The
Fleet *(RKO, 1936).*

The last few months of 1935 and the early months
of 1936 were both happy and sad ones for Fred.
Happy because of the huge success of *Top Hat*
(released in September) and the birth of his son
Fred Jr , sad because in the very month that *Top
Hat* opened, Adele gave birth to twin boys who
both died. It was a tragedy for Adele who had
desperately wanted to have and enjoy children,
children she at last realised she would never have.

And as if Fred hadn't got enough on his
schedule he decided to try his luck at the medium
of radio. He acted as a linkman and singer on a
radio series called *The Hit Parade*. It was spon-
sored by Lucky Strike cigarettes and Fred plugged
not only the *Top Hat* songs for all his worth but
also several other top songs that were selling well
in the record stores. He even danced a bit at the
end of each show although quite what the radio
audience thought of the sound of tapping feet
coming from their sets is hard to imagine.

Still, they didn't have to wait long for the real
thing. In 1935 Fred and Ginger had danced
together twice. In 1936 they were to do the same in
the films *Follow The Fleet* and *Swing Time*. RKO
was certainly getting its mileage out of the two
performers. In fact, as far as Fred was concerned,
they were beginning to get too much mileage, at
least for what they were paying.

He and Ginger had only to point to the list of
moneymaking stars that was published annually in
Hollywood. As the list for the top ten of 1935 was
released Fred and Ginger went straight in at
number four. Only Shirley Temple, Will Rogers
and Clark Gable were ahead of them. The same
thing happened in 1936, except that Fred and
Ginger moved up to third place.

Fred began to campaign for more money. He
was still on much the same contract he had signed
when making *Flying Down To Rio* some three years
earlier. That had stipulated that he received $1500
a week with options of additional weekly sums of
$500 while making a film. They were fair terms
considering his stature as a performer in 1933.
They were not, however, good enough for a star
whose musical genius and dancing talent were
keeping RKO solvent.

Fred, of course, wasn't the only star who was
beginning to question the terms of his contract.
Stars at other studios were also starting to rebel,

Right: Follow The
Fleet, *the second of the
three Astaire/Rogers
RKO musicals written
by Irving Berlin in the
1930s. The others –*
Top Hat *(1935) and*
Carefree *(1938).*

Above: *A more relaxed Fred with co-star Randolph Scott dreaming of the two women in their lives – Ginger Rogers and Harriet Hilliard.* Follow The Fleet *(RKO, 1936).*

Right: *Champs! Fred and Ginger come out top in the Paradise Ballroom contest with their interpretation of 'Let Yourself Go!',* Follow The Fleet *(RKO, 1936).*

Opposite: *Fourteen takes before they got it right and then they used take one! The elegant 'Let's Face The Music And Dance' number from* Follow The Fleet *(RKO, 1936).*

55

Victor Moore, Fred and
director George Stevens
'between takes' on the set
of the 1936 classic Swing
Time (RKO).

'Bojangles of Harlem',
the tribute by Fred and
choreographer Hermes
Pan to Bill Robinson in
Swing Time (RKO,
1936).

some over better terms, others over the quality of their material. Bette Davis at Warner Bros was the most famous example. She left Hollywood and fled to England when Jack Warner offered her a role in a movie called *God's Country And The Woman*, a lumberjack story told in Technicolor. Bette had just won an Oscar and felt that a lumberjack story wasn't really up to the mark. She fought against her contract in the English courts. She lost and had to return to Hollywood and eat humble pie but the publicity was such that Warner had to make sure she received roles that were worthy of her undoubted talents.

Fred wasn't complaining on that score. His roles were fine. He had his own personal freedom to experiment with dance routines, he had a string of top composers lining up to work for him and he had a friendly and relaxed atmosphere in which to work. It was just that he wanted more money. And he deserved it.

When talks eventually got under way at RKO the press began to speculate about Fred leaving RKO if things didn't work out. Or that he and Ginger might at last split up. The negotiations were kept secret but all kinds of rumours began flying about, not least the one that Fred had turned down a $400,000 deal for each of eight new pictures. Eventually, when it was all settled, the terms of the deal were not released although many Hollywood columnists felt that the $400,000 deal that had been mooted was not too wide of the mark. As for Ginger? She was given an assurance that she would not be required to make more than two pictures a year with Fred and that she would be allowed to star in an additional two pictures of her own.

Follow The Fleet, the first of the two films they made in 1936, again had a score by Irving Berlin. It was a remake of an old silent called *Shore Leave* which had already been remade once six years earlier as *Hit The Deck*. Fred played an ex-hoofer turned sailor who meets up again with his former dancing partner Ginger and, together with Harriet Hilliard and sailor Randolph Scott, put on a show to save a ship.

The sight of Fred in bell-bottoms was at least

'Bojangles of Harlem' from Swing Time *(RKO, 1936). The number marked the only occasion that Fred appeared in blackface on screen.*

Right: *A snowy park. Ginger in caracul coat. Fred complete with bowler. Result? 'A Fine Romance!'*, Swing Time *(RKO, 1936).*

Opposite: *Fred and Ginger and the fast-paced 'Pick Yourself Up' in George Stevens'* Swing Time *(RKO, 1936).*

'Waltz In Swing Time' — two and a half minutes of musical perfection shot in just one take. A highlight of the 1936 musical Swing Time *(RKO).*

something new but there was no disguising the fact that *Follow The Fleet* was not the most distinguished of Astaire/Rogers musicals even though Berlin came up with seven new songs for the picture.

Once again Fred and Ginger found one of the numbers troublesome. The song in question was the classic 'Let's Face The Music And Dance', the climactic number of the picture. As usual Fred was dressed in a dinner suit. Ginger on this occasion wore a sparkling full-length gown with a fur collar. During the first take Fred was hit in the eye with a piece of Ginger's dress or sleeve. The result was that for the rest of the sequence Fred could hardly see and moved around more or less by instinct. To no-one's surprise he asked for them to do it again. Ginger said 'sure', the clapperboard boy cried 'take two' and off they went again.

None of this of course was a rehearsal. It was for real and costing time and money. By the time Fred and Ginger had danced 'Let's Face The Music And Dance' 14 times the song's title was beginning to have some relevance for everyone connected with

The trade advertisement for Shall We Dance? *(1937), Fred and Ginger's seventh film together at RKO.*

FRED ASTAIRE GINGER ROGERS
"SHALL WE DANCE"

with
EDWARD EVERETT HORTON · ERIC BLORE · JEROME COWAN
KETTI GALLIAN · WILLIAM BRISBANE and HARRIET HOCTOR

Above: *The lobby card for Fred and Ginger's 1937 Gershwin hit* Shall We Dance? *(RKO).*

Left: *No top hat, white tie or tails. Instead casual wear and the hissing engine-room of a ship. But the result is still the same — perfection. Fred's 'Slap That Bass' solo in* Shall We Dance? *(RKO, 1937).*

Left: *Fred and Ginger roller skate to 'Let's Call The Whole Thing Off' in* Shall We Dance? *(RKO, 1937).*

the shooting. Eventually, at around eight o'clock at night, Fred agreed to call a halt and suggested that they all get together and take a look at what they'd got the next morning. When the next morning came and Fred decided on which take to use he chose take one. There's no record of what Ginger had to say, but Fred commented: 'I wasted eight hours of my past life for something we already had.'

The other numbers in *Follow The Fleet* included 'I'd Rather Lead A Band', a solo tap dance by Fred, 'Let Yourself Go' sung by Ginger (and subsequently danced by Fred and Ginger) in a ballroom contest and the memorable 'I'm Putting All My Eggs In One Basket', introduced by Fred at the piano and then danced by both him and Ginger in one of their competitive 'Anything You Can Do I Can Do Better' routines.

This last number is zany, captivating fun with Fred and Ginger trying to outhoof each other every step of the way. Hermes Pan once again worked with Fred as dance director: 'Sometimes from kidding around one gag leads to an idea. So in the "I'm Putting All My Eggs In One Basket" routine we hit on the idea of Ginger getting stuck in a step. Fred and she would start to dance and then Ginger couldn't get out of it, and he would give her a nudge and she would catch up with him. Then he would go along to a certain place and she would get stuck again and he would come up again and bump Ginger to get her out of the stuck needle bit. It was rather fun, and is the sort of thing you don't really plan.'

After *Top Hat*, the critics were a bit lukewarm in their attitudes towards *Follow The Fleet* but the picture still managed to garner some good notices ('Even though it is not the best of their series, it still is good enough to take the head of this year's class in song and dance entertainment,' said *The New York Times*) and, more important as far as RKO was concerned, it made money. The queues still wound their way round the blocks to see Fred Astaire and Ginger Rogers.

Swing Time was a vast improvement all round. The plot had Fred as a gambler/dancer who goes to New York to win $25,000 and be worthy of the girl he has left back home but who meets up with the delicious Ginger instead. The film's director was not Mark Sandrich who had directed three of Fred and Ginger's five films together but George Stevens whose first musical this was.

Stevens was later to become one of the Holly-wood greats with films such as *Shane* and *Giant*. Just a year before *Swing Time* he had been no more than a contract director at RKO, working on low budget comedies. But then a property called *Alice Adams* came up. It was a Booth Tarkington story and was set to star Katharine Hepburn. Pandro Berman had two directors in mind, both of them young. One was William Wyler who had already earned a reputation for himself in Hollywood, the other was the unknown Stevens whose career Berman thought was just about to 'pop'. Berman was willing to give Stevens a chance not least because he was on the RKO payroll and was cheaper than Wyler. The die was cast in Berman's office around six o'clock one evening. After long discussions with Hepburn about who should direct

Opposite: *Ballet dancer Fred falls for musical comedy star Ginger. The plot didn't matter but as always the music, by the Gershwins, did.* Shall We Dance? *(RKO, 1937).*

HERE THEY COME . . . in the grandest,
gayest, laughingest musical show of all
. . . With Fred topping his top in the
DRUM DANCE, that dancing sensation
of sensations . . . and George and Gracie
gracier than ever . . . as romance and
rhythm and fun run
riot on a screen
alive with the lift of
GERSHWIN music
and WODEHOUSE
humor!

FRED ASTAIRE
GEORGE BURNS and GRACIE ALLEN

"A Damsel in Distress"

with
JOAN FONTAINE
REGINALD GARDINER · RAY NOBLE
CONSTANCE COLLIER · MONTAGU LOVE · HARRY WATSON

Music by GEORGE GERSHWIN · Lyrics by IRA GERSHWIN
From the story by P. G. WODEHOUSE

Thrill to 4 new song hits...

"Foggy Day"—"Nice
Work If You Can Get It"—
"Things Are Looking Up"—
"I Can't Be Bothered Now"

A PANDRO S. BERMAN PRODUCTION
DIRECTED BY GEORGE STEVENS

they agreed to toss a coin. Heads for Wyler, tails for Stevens. It came down heads. Hepburn looked at Berman. Berman looked at Hepburn. Berman said: 'How about tossing it again?' She said: 'fine'. So they tossed it. It came down tails and they took George Stevens. And that's how one of the great careers of Hollywood got started – on the second toss of a coin.

The story has nothing to do with Fred Astaire of course other than without that lucky flip Stevens would not have directed *Swing Time*. But it does illustrate just how much luck as well as talent had a part to play in getting careers started in those early sound days of Hollywood. It also illustrates what a happy-go-lucky outfit RKO was. No flip of the coin would have decided the career of a director at Metro or Paramount or Warners.

Swing Time which was originally entitled *Never Gonna Dance* (one of the songs included in the picture) contains one of the finest numbers Fred ever danced to on screen – 'Bojangles Of Harlem', a jazzy tribute to the great tap dancer Bill 'Bojan-

gles' Robinson. It was the first and only time that Fred appeared with a blackened face. The number introduced Fred to the possibilities of combining dance with trick and process photography. It was something he was to pursue with great success later in his career.

The number opens with Fred performing nimbly with a line of chorus girls dressed in black and white. It then continues with him alone against a white backcloth. As he begins to dance three huge silhouettes of his dancing form, each of them five times his size, appear behind him. To start with they dance with him in perfect synchronisation but as he starts to make the steps more complicated they begin to lose time. His steps become more and more involved and in the end the three shadows give up trying to compete and stomp off in disgust. Dominated by a set which incorporated two huge shoes, the number belongs with the most inventive things Fred ever did on the RKO sound stages.

Other routines in the picture included 'Waltz In Swing Time' danced by Fred and Ginger to

varying tempos and rhythms, 'Pick Yourself Up' performed on the bare boards of a practice room, the lyrical 'Never Gonna Dance', 'A Fine Romance' set in a snowy park, and 'The Way You Look Tonight' which was sung by Fred at the piano to Ginger with her hair covered in shampoo. The song, written like the others in the picture by Jerome Kern and Dorothy Fields, became the second song performed by Fred to win an Oscar in the 1930s.

Fred and Ginger spent something like 350 hours rehearsing their numbers for *Swing Time*. Said Ginger: 'The first hundred hours are the most difficult because they are the kindergarten course for the new routines. Once the new steps are learned it becomes more fascinating to fit them together and perfect the execution of the routines.'

George Stevens for one was amazed at the hours Fred and Ginger spent rehearsing. He was not used to musical films and remembered how, one evening after Fred and Ginger had been working on a very difficult routine, he walked across the empty stage to a prop man who was getting ready to mop the floor. The time was eight in the evening

Fred with his only other RKO leading lady of the 1930s, Joan Fontaine. The song – 'Things Are Looking Up'. The film – A Damsel In Distress (RKO, 1937).

Fred with George Burns and Gracie Allen, plus distorting fairground mirrors, in the 'Stiff Upper Lip' number in A Damsel In Distress (RKO, 1937).

LET RHYTHM RING! . . . FRED AND GINGER ARE BACK AGAIN
FRED ASTAIRE GINGER ROGERS
"CAREFREE"

MOVIE QUIZ $250,000.00 CONTEST PICTURES

COUNTRY OF ORIGIN U. S. A

The art deco style lobby card for Carefree, *a style much in vogue in Hollywoood in the 1930s.*

and Stevens asked the man what he was doing. The prop man pointed down. There was blood on the floor. Ginger's feet had blistered during the dozens of takes. She had never said a word and carried on dancing. The blood eventually seeped through the soles of her shoes and stained the floor.

Such hardships, of course, went unnoticed by the critics and the public. They were interested only in what was up there on the screen. And what they saw in *Swing Time* they liked. There are many, in fact, who consider the film as good if not better than *Top Hat*. Wrote one New York critic: 'If by any chance you are harbouring any fears that Mr Astaire and Miss Rogers have lost their magnificent sense of rhythm be reassured. Their routines still exemplify ballroom technique at its best.' Said another: 'They have never performed with more exquisite finish.'

By 1937 it was that last word 'finish' that was beginning to worry those in charge at RKO. Berman knew regrettably that sooner or later the Astaire/Rogers team would have to split up. The rumours abounded in the press. Fred would like to go it alone or Ginger wanted to dance no more and so on. Berman said: 'I realise that very soon I've got to face the certainty of breaking up my team.'

Before any plans for the next production could be realised Fred took a holiday to England with Phyllis. On the way he stopped off in New York and did six 15-minute radio shows at $4000 a piece. The holiday was a rushed one. He saw Adele, stayed at Claridges and gave one interview to Britain's leading film critic C. A. Lejeune in $3\frac{1}{2}$ minutes flat. On the way back he had another shot at radio, this time involving himself in no fewer than 39 shows for the Packard Motor Show. He sang and danced in front of the mike, putting almost as much effort into performing for the mike as he did when practising his movie routines.

But after 39 shows he'd had enough. Phyllis saw he was knocking himself out and with the programmes beginning to intrude on the rehearsals for his next film, *Shall We Dance?*, he decided to stop radio shows.

The critics were kind to *Shall We Dance?* (1937) directed once again by Mark Sandrich. Frank Nugent wrote in *The New York Times*: 'One of the best things the screen's premier dance team has done, a zestful, prancing, sophisticated musical show. It has a grand score by George Gershwin (lyrics by brother Ira), a generous leavening of comedy, a plot or so and, forever, and ever, the

Fred and Ginger perform 'The Yam' in their 1938 musical Carefree *(RKO).*

EDNA MAY OLIVER · WALTER BRENNAN

Above: *The announcement of Fred and Ginger's last film together for RKO,* The Story of Vernon And Irene Castle, *the only film in which they portrayed real people – the Castles, the king and queen of ballroom dancing (RKO, 1939).*

nimble hoofing of a chap with quicksilver in his feet and of a young woman who has leapt to follow him with assurance.'

The public on the other end were, for the very first time, less than enthusiastic. The picture made a profit all right – $413,000 – but it was not the kind of profit usually made by RKO from the Astaire/Rogers ventures. And in just one more year, 1938, Fred and Ginger would appear in a film called *Carefree* that, for the first time actually lost money – $68,000. The writing was on the wall and secretly everyone, from Fred and Ginger down, knew it.

One of the problems was trying to come up with new routines. After five years together Fred and Ginger had danced just about every step, in every setting and through every corny story the RKO writers could dream up. The thing that kept Fred going was not so much his routines with Ginger which were perfection as always but his solo numbers. When he was on his own with a single prop or a gimmick he could at least try something new.

In *Shall We Dance?* for instance he performed a number called 'Slap That Bass' in a machine room on board ship, moving and tapping his way through the sequence to the accompaniment of hissing pistons and revolving naval machinery. It wasn't a number that he had planned, but had come

about by accident as he was walking with Hermes Pan across the RKO lot after lunch. As they strolled back to the stages they passed a cement mixer that was being used for construction work. The mixer was making a monotonous but rhythmic kind of noise and as he heard it Fred began to move slowly to its rhythm. From that single everyday experience came one of Fred's best-ever solo routines.

Similarly, his 'Since They Turned Loch Lomond Into Swing' in *Carefree* is built entirely round Fred teeing off and dancing with a golf club. The number is breathtaking in its precision especially as it comes to its climax when Fred, dancing and tapping before each stroke, sends 5 golf balls down the fairway. Fred supposedly spent 2 weeks on the routine and used up 600 golf balls in the process.

In *Shall We Dance?* he even danced with Ginger on roller skates to the 'Let's Call The Whole Thing Off' number, a sequence that involved 4 days' shooting and director Sandrich shouting 'action' 150 times as they put together the 2-minute 40-second number.

But the gimmicks had about them a hint of desperation. With each succeeding film Fred and his choreographer were under increasing pressure to produce new ideas. They knew that the public would be comparing what they did now with what

Opposite: *Still making the front cover even in 1939. Fred and Ginger pictured just a month before the release of their last film together at RKO.*

STAGE

THE MAGAZINE OF

After Dark

35¢

Fred Astaire and Ginger Rogers
as Vernon and Irene Castle
in the R K O — Radio picture,
The Castles

FEBRUARY
1939

had gone before. It was both a strain and a worry.

The same problem befell Gene Kelly in the mid-1950s when he had run his course at the mighty MGM. In the last film he made during his most creative period at the studio – *It's Always Fair Weather* – Gene danced on roller skates, just as Fred and Ginger danced on roller skates at RKO in 1937. Roller skates, it seemed, were the ultimate solution when all else failed. But at least Fred never got round to dancing with a dustbin lid attached to his foot as did Messrs Kelly, Dan Dailey and Michael Kidd in *It's Always Fair Weather*. That really *did* seem like desperation.

The last two pictures Fred and Ginger made together at RKO were *Carefree* and *The Story Of Vernon And Irene Castle* (1939). Just before the making of the two films Fred also embarked on his first musical without Ginger (who had asked for a break) – *A Damsel In Distress* (1937).

Directed again by George Stevens, it turned out to be one of Fred's best. His role was of an American dancer in England who tries to woo and wed an aristocratic British lady living in a castle. The lady was played by Joan Fontaine who certainly managed to give off an aristocratic air. But she was no dancer and simply strolled with Fred through one of the songs.

In fact, just about the only thing wrong with *A Damsel In Distress* was that Ginger wasn't in it. For the rest, the score by the Gershwins was superb and the comedy of George Burns and Gracie Allen, brought over by RKO from Paramount to try to help compensate for Ginger's loss, was impeccable.

The numbers included 'A Foggy Day', 'Put Me To The Test' and 'Nice Work If You Can Get It', in which Fred pounded away with verve and enthusiasm on every percussion instrument in sight. Other songs were 'I Can't Be Bothered Now' (sung by Fred on a London street) and 'Stiff Upper Lip', performed by Fred and Burns and Allen in a fairground in which the three of them abandon themselves in a funhouse full of distorted mirrors.

Carefree, as well as registering as the first Astaire/Rogers 'loser' also marked the first occasion the pair kissed on screen. Fred had never thought it necessary in any of their films and in view of the fact that the film finished up in the 'loss' column of the RKO ledgers perhaps they shouldn't have done it!

The film had Ginger as a radio singer who can't make up her mind about marriage. She goes to psychiatrist Fred for help, with the inevitable result. The songs were once more by Irving Berlin. They included not only the aforementioned 'Since They Turned Loch Lomond Into Swing' but also the bewitching 'Change Partners' performed by Fred and Ginger on a flagstone terrace, 'I Used To Be Colour Blind' (originally planned as a Technicolor number), a dream sequence set among lush decor and which ends in lyrical slow motion, and 'The Yam', a country club number which incorporated just about all of Fred and

Ginger's best movements together and climaxed with a series of exhilarating lifts.

As if to emphasise that it was at last time for Fred and Ginger to part, their final film together, *The Story Of Vernon And Irene Castle*, also lost money. After the film's release RKO were $50,000 out of pocket. The picture was the first they had made together based on the lives of real people, namely the famous couple who made ballroom dancing so popular throughout the world before the First World War. RKO, aware that the film was the last in which Fred and Ginger were to appear, extracted every ounce of sweat and imagination from their publicity department: 'Exciting! Thrilling! Beautiful! A story written by life and events to be played *only* by Fred and Ginger! . . . The true-life romance of the couple who made dancing the world's favourite pastime! . . . A story that will leave you limp with *tears* . . . and gloriously glowing with a great Cavalcade of the Dance, recreating the Castle Walk, the Maxixe, the Tango, the Texas Tommy! . . . All the gaieties and glories, the swift drama and glamorous pageantry of a warmly-remembered yesterday, parading before your eyes!'

In 1939 the 'warmly remembered yesterday' belonged not only to Vernon and Irene Castle but also to Fred and Ginger. It was estimated that, during the 1930s, 125,000 feet of dancing film had been recorded on their pictures and that of this approximately 75,000 were printed and 25,000 feet used in their movies. Another statistic was that creating, rehearsing and filming dances in the Astaire/Rogers pictures worked out at something like 500 hours per film.

Perhaps the most important statistic of all was that between them Fred and Ginger had kept a major Hollywood studio afloat almost entirely by their own efforts. They weren't the only ones to have done so in the 1930s – Mae West's sexual innuendos had helped save Paramount, Shirley Temple had done wonders for Twentieth Century-Fox while Zanuck searched frantically around for stars and Deanna Durbin sang her heart out to keep Universal in business – but Fred and Ginger were the only ones to have achieved it through dance.

In 1939 Fred was listed as one of America's richest men. Top of the heap was William Randolph Hearst whose earnings came out somewhere in the $500,000 a year mark. Fred was listed fifth. Not bad going for the man who had been dismissed with that screen test some ten years earlier!

The abiding memory of Fred and Ginger in the 1930s is of Fred dressed in white tie and tails, and Ginger in satin or silk waltzing and tapping their way across what, in memory at least, seems like hundreds of marble ballrooms. One number merges into another until sometimes one can't quite remember which number belongs to which film. But that matters little. The important thing is that they did dance together and that they did it so brilliantly for so long.

CHANGE PARTNERS

The first thing Fred decided on after his long years at RKO was a vacation. He had been promising Phyllis another trip to Europe for many years and with the end of the RKO films he at last had a chance to fulfil that promise.

The European tour certainly relaxed him. He met up again with Adele in Ireland and managed to enjoy plenty of horse racing, fishing and golf. The trouble with Fred was that he just couldn't be away from things for too long without anxieties beginning to nag away at him. The questions most constantly on his mind were: 'What was he going to do next?' 'Should he retire?' 'Was he too old (in May 1939 he was 40) to carry on dancing on screen?' On top of everything he was missing his son Fred Jr and Phyllis' son Peter who was away at boarding-school.

Fred enjoyed the holiday but in many ways he wasn't too sorry when it came to an end. He decided against retirement (to retire or not was a question that was to come up regularly in the years ahead) and opted to make a movie at MGM, *The Broadway Melody Of 1940*. Phyllis was of the opinion that a film based on the life of the Russian

The lobby card for Broadway Melody Of 1940, *Fred's first starring film at Metro-Goldwyn-Mayer.*

ballet dancer Nijinsky (another possible project) would show his dancing skills to better advantage but there was no dissuading Fred. He headed firmly in the direction of the giant musical stages of MGM, Hollywood's greatest studio.

Fred, of course, had been at MGM before for just a few days in 1933 in *Dancing Lady* but in 1940 he arrived not as 'Fred Astaire, the dancer' but 'Fred Astaire, the star'. There were many who felt that Metro was the studio at which he should have been all along and there's little doubt that if Louis B. Mayer could have enticed him away from the RKO studios in the 1930s he would certainly have done so.

But 1940 was, in many ways, the best time for Fred to start taking a close look at that famous studio. For the first time MGM was beginning to dominate the screen musical and although no-one realised it at the time it was a domination that was to last uninterrupted for almost 20 years. Mind you, anyone closely connected with the Hollywood scene could see clearly how the studio was building

Above: *Fred and Eleanor Powell rehearse before a large mirror at MGM's Culver City studios while preparing for* Broadway Melody Of 1940 *(MGM, 1940)*.

Right: *Fred and Eleanor Powell 'get with it' in* Broadway Melody Of 1940, *directed by Norman Taurog (MGM, 1940)*.

Opposite: *Cole Porter's 'Begin The Beguine'. George Murphy, Eleanor Powell and Fred share the finale of* Broadway Melody Of 1940 *(MGM, 1940)*.

SECOND CHORUS

its musical team. Song-writer Arthur Freed had become a producer, composer-arranger Roger Edens was a permanent fixture, Judy Garland and Mickey Rooney were teaming together, Busby Berkeley had left Warners for MGM. Vincente Minnelli was soon to arrive. As was Gene Kelly. Fred too was to become a part of that dazzling line-up but not for a little while. In 1940 he was content with just the one movie at Metro.

The Broadway Melody Of 1940 was the third and last of the *Broadway Melody* series begun by MGM back in the late 1930s. It starred Fred and George Murphy as a couple of hoofers down on their luck who are spotted by a Broadway pro-ducer. The producer wants Fred for his new show but, because of a case of mistaken identity, finishes up with Murphy instead. It was a trivial mix-up tale in which all comes right in the end and which was really no different from those Fred had been appearing in at RKO. The one big difference, however, was that instead of dancing with Ginger Rogers, Fred teamed with Eleanor Powell.

With Fred, Eleanor Powell was something special. Indeed, purely as a dancer, she was something special without him. When she made her screen debut in a guest spot in Fox's *George White's Scandals* in 1935 she was cited by The

Dancing Masters Of America as 'the world's greatest tap dancer'. But, as MGM discovered when they signed her the following year, she tended to lack personality and also, in their words, 'femininity' which they tried hard to put to rights with their huge army of beauticians. But Eleanor Powell stubbornly remained Eleanor Powell, a superb dancer, a so-so actress and a long, long way from the usual kind of glamour girl found on the MGM lot. Roger Edens who worked with her at the studio said that 'She had a certain unusual quality that was very fresh and appealing and she could certainly dance.'

And she certainly proved it in *The Broadway Melody Of 1940* which MGM promoted with the slogan 'The World's Greatest Dancers In The World's Greatest Musical Show!'

It wasn't that exactly but it did have its great moments, notably when Fred joined Eleanor in a rendering of Cole Porter's 'Begin The Beguine'. In the first of the two *That's Entertainment* films of the 1970s the sequence is introduced by Frank Sinatra who advises the audience: 'Take a good look at this scene folks, you won't see its like again.' And indeed it's doubtful that we ever will.

First heard in Porter's 1935 Broadway musical *Jubilee*, the number cost $120,000 to stage. Photo-graphed in sharply contrasting black and white and danced on a glittering, mirrored floor against a starry background, it is introduced by a sultry vocal after which Fred and Eleanor go into a speciality routine. The tempo is changed once more, this time by a vocal quartet, Andrews Sisters style, and then Fred and Eleanor, dressed in white, appear for a second time, building the number to an exhilarating climax and tapping for what seems like forever without musical accompani-ment. The result is sheer magic, two artists at their peak, playing with and interpreting a memorable song with their twinkling feet. In anybody's top ten list of Fred Astaire numbers, his 'Begin The Beguine' with Eleanor Powell would be certain of inclusion.

Cole Porter was also responsible for the rest of the film's score which included Eleanor's ship-board 'I Am The Captain', Fred and George Murphy engaging in a pleasing little vaudeville routine 'Please Don't Monkey With Broadway', the lyrical 'Between You And Me' which allowed Murphy and Powell to get together, 'Juke Box Dance' performed by Fred and Eleanor to a boogie-woogie beat and Fred's 'I've Got My Eyes On You' in which he dances on an empty stage using a sheet music photograph of Eleanor as his

Above: *Fred and Paulette Goddard in full flow. A scene from the 1940 Paramount musical* Second Chorus.

Opposite top: *The lobby card for Paramount's* Second Chorus *in which Fred danced with Charlie Chaplin's protégée Paulette Goddard.*

Opposite bottom: Second Chorus *(1940), Fred's first film at Paramount. A publicity still with his co-star Paulette Goddard.*

partner. All, in their own ways, were excellent numbers, especially the last but none came close to the magic and perfection of the magnificent 'Begin The Beguine'.

When *The Broadway Melody Of 1940* opened at the Capitol, New York in March 1940, *The New York Times* found it appreciably superior to the previous films in the series and mentioned that 'Fred's arabesques seemed even more fascinatingly intricate than ever'. But by then Fred was less concerned with the opulence of lavish MGM musicals than he was with the news from Britain, which had been at war with Germany for over six months and, with Europe overrun by the Nazis, had its back to the wall.

Many stars, Fred's long-time friend David Niven among them, had returned to Britain to serve in the forces and those Britons who remained behind felt more than a little twinge of guilt about staying in sunny California when Britain was almost on its knees.

Fred's concern, of course, was for the safety of

Above: *Jazz trumpeters Fred Astaire and Burgess Meredith, plus the Artie Shaw band. Three of the key ingredients of* Second Chorus *(Paramount, 1940).*

Right: *Fred with the 23-year-old Rita Hayworth, regarded by many critics as his best-ever dancing partner. The film, the first of the two they made together,* You'll Never Get Rich *(Columbia, 1941).*

Opposite: *'Wedding Cake Walk'. Fred and Rita Hayworth in Columbia's* You'll Never Get Rich *(1941).*

They could pull out all
the stops even at little
Columbia when it came to
a Fred Astaire musical.
The grand finale to
You'll Never Get Rich
(1941).

Right: *Fred – dance director turned soldier – in* You'll Never Get Rich *(Columbia, 1941)*.

Below: *An irresistible combination – Fred and Rita Hayworth and the exquisite 'So Near And Yet So Far' number in* You'll Never Get Rich *(Columbia, 1941)*.

Adele. During those early harrowing days of the Second World War he kept in constant touch with her, checking that she was all right and asking if there was anything he or their mother could do. What their mother did was send her a large parcel of dried Californian fruit, a service she continued regularly to carry out. Fred also did his best to keep in touch with all his English friends and associates and wrote not only to his show business acquaintances but also to people like George Griffin who at one time had been his valet in London.

The war unsettled Fred and in the early 1940s he became decidedly footloose as far as his career was concerned. He found it difficult to think about movies seriously and was unable to settle at one studio. One thing he was certain of, however. He was not looking for a new and regular dancing partner even though the gossip columns were constantly raising the question: 'Who's going to be the new Ginger?' As far as Fred was concerned, *no-one* was going to be the new Ginger. In fact for the rest of his dancing career he never danced with a leading lady more than twice, not even Rita Hayworth or Cyd Charisse.

Some he danced with only once. And one of those was Paulette Goddard. Just why Fred signed up with Paramount to make a musical called *Second Chorus* (1940) is difficult now to fathom. It would have been understandable if he had moved across to Warners who had always had a strong musical tradition and where James Cagney was soon to take everyone's breath away by singing and dancing through *Yankee Doodle Dandy*. And even Twentieth Century-Fox who were then becoming involved in a long line of Betty Grable musicals might have offered more opportunities. But Paramount was very definitely not the top musical studio in town as Fred found to his cost after making *Second Chorus*.

If 'Begin The Beguine' in *The Broadway Melody* had been an Astaire 'high' then just about all of *Second Chorus* ranked as a 'low'. Even Fred's old colleague Hermes Pan who worked as dance director on the picture couldn't make anything come to life. Paulette Goddard had long slim legs and she looked attractive in sheer black tights but she was no dancer. She was better off with Charlie Chaplin (for whom she had made *Modern Times*

and *The Great Dictator*) than she was in a musical about a couple of jazz trumpeters (Fred and Burgess Meredith) who vie for her affections.

Second Chance was a sorry mess. Fred performed just three times and then only briefly – first with Goddard in the fast 'I Ain't Hep To That Step But I'll Dig It', then in a solo spoof of a Russian squat-dancer and finally in another solo as the light-footed leader of the band. The music came from a wide variety of composers and lyricists – Artie Shaw, Victor Young, Johnny Mercer and Hal Borne, E. Y. Harburg and Johnny Green. Between them they should at least have come up with something serviceable. As it was, the Artie Shaw band came out of things the best.

In *The New York Times* Bosley Crowther made his views patently clear: 'There is no getting around it: Fred Astaire is still badly in need of a new dancing partner. And, judging by *Second Chorus*, he is even more desperately in need of a producer, writers and a director who will again stir up something smart, sleek and joyous for him to do. For seldom has a first class talent been less effectively used ... and seldom has more flat,

You need to look carefully at Fred's co-star in this scene. Close examination reveals Bing Crosby in a sequence from the 1942 Paramount production Holiday Inn.

Rita begins to suspect that down-on-his-luck dancer Fred may be a secret admirer. A scene from You Were Never Lovelier *(Columbia, 1942).*

routine material been labelled top flight musical comedy than it is in this slaphazard picture.'

It was the worst notice that one of Fred's films had ever received. And it was ironic that *Second Chorus* should be released just a week after a film called *Kitty Foyle* had opened at the Rivoli in New York. *Kitty Foyle* was a tear-jerker. It was all about a girl from the wrong side of the tracks who falls for a handsome socialite but eventually finds true happiness with a man from her own level of society. There wasn't a musical number in it. Its star was Ginger Rogers. And for her role she was named best actress of 1940 by the Oscar Academy.

Still, even though Fred was temporarily down and Ginger was riding the crest of the Hollywood wave, it wouldn't be long before Fred would again find success. Early in 1941 he signed with Columbia Pictures to make a couple of films with a young actress who very soon was to become one of the top pin-ups of the war years. Her name was Rita Hayworth.

Years later, at a San Francisco Film Festival, Rita remembered her two films with Fred at Columbia with more than a little affection: 'I guess the jewels of my life were the pictures I made with Fred Astaire,' she said. 'When he came to do the two films at Columbia, he *asked* for me. Fred knew I was a dancer. He *knew* what all those dumb-dumbs at Columbia didn't know, and if it hadn't been for him I wouldn't have been cast in either film.'

She was right in saying that the jewels in her life were the Astaire pictures but she was wrong when she said that Fred had asked for her and that the people running Columbia were dumb-dumbs.

Harry Cohn, the Columbia studio boss, may have been rough and tough and the crudest talking man in town. And he was not exactly the most educated man in the world. But he was not dumb. And he was a good businessman.

But in 1941 he did find himself in something of a spot. Frank Capra, the director who had taken Columbia from being just another studio on Poverty Row and with his social comedies made it a force to be reckoned with, had left the studio and Cohn found himself in charge of the 22-year-old Rita and without an idea in his head about how best to use her. He knew she was musical because her father had been a well-known Spanish dancer and Rita's first appearance on film (as Rita Cansino)

Fred auditions on the desk of hotel owner Adolphe Menjou. An early scene from Columbia's 1942 musical You Were Never Lovelier.

87

had been as a slinky tango dancer in the 1935 Fox movie *Dante's Inferno*. But since 1937, the year she had signed with Columbia, she had appeared in over 20 films and there hadn't been a musical among them. It was only because of her performance as the sexually tormenting wife of pilot Richard Barthelmess in Howard Hawks' *Only Angels Have Wings* that she had come to the attention of the public.

After her success in the Hawks picture Cohn decided that the best way he could capitalise on Rita's physical beauty and musical talents was by lending her to other studios, but so successful was she in movies like *Blood And Sand*, a bullfighting drama starring Tyrone Power, and *The Strawberry Blonde* in which she featured with James Cagney at Warners that Cohn revised his plans and began preparing properties for her at Columbia.

The trouble was the studio wasn't musical. And, apart from producing a few semi-successful Grace Moore vehicles back in the 1930s, it never had been. So Cohn began importing musical talent and that's where Fred came into the scheme of things.

Fred arrived at Columbia not because he walked into Cohn's office and asked for Rita but because Cohn approached Fred and suggested that he make a couple of movies with his new star, Rita Hayworth.

Fred had known Rita's father Eduardo back in the vaudeville days some 30 years earlier so he had little doubt that Rita could dance. He knew too that she would have had excellent training and that it might be fun to draw some of her talent out. Her height of five feet six inches might be a problem (Fred was five feet nine and three-quarter inches) but low heels would almost certainly cure that. As for Rita, she was both thrilled and terrified at the prospect of dancing with Fred: 'I went to meet him in the studio and there was no-one else there. I was so shy I couldn't even say his name. He talked to me and said, "Well, let's try to do these little steps," so I tried to follow him and figure it out. He was amazed, he said, "How can you do that so fast? Of course I know why, it's because your training is excellent from your father." I said, "Well yes, I've been dancing since I was three or four years old."'

Fred in the lavish 'If Swing Goes, I Go Too' number from Ziegfeld Follies *(MGM, 1945). Like several other sequences in the film it did indeed 'go' and was cut from the final release print.*

Rita later added: 'Dancing is my natural heritage, and I have always loved it. But I always hated to practise. Rehearsals with Fred Astaire, however, were occasions I found myself looking forward to with an anticipation of pleasure.'

Cohn, anxious to make Rita's first musical at Columbia an impressive one, brought in not only Fred but also Cole Porter who composed seven songs for the movie which Cohn titled *You'll Never Get Rich*. Fred played a Broadway dance director who gets drafted, Rita played the beautiful chorus girl he was after from reel one.

Fred enjoyed making *You'll Never Get Rich* because it was one of the first films with a Second World War service background. Cole Porter didn't enjoy it quite as much. He was used to writing songs for films with more elegant themes and found it difficult composing numbers for a film that revolved around military life. He was also used to bigger Hollywood outfits than Columbia and was first amused and then not a little disconcerted when Harry Cohn insisted on submitting his songs to clerical workers in order to 'pretest' their appeal.

The songs included 'So Near And Yet So Far' and 'Boogie Woogie Barcarolle', danced by both Fred and Rita, and the huge production number 'Wedding Cake Walk' which was staged by Robert Alton on a set featuring a 50-strong chorus line and a giant wedding cake topped by a tank!

Fred also enjoyed himself with a bevy of beautiful chorus girls in the 'Shootin' The Works For Uncle Sam' number and in 'The A-stairable Rag' in which he was backed by the Delta Rhythm Boys – Buddy Colette on clarinet, A. Grant on guitar, Chico Hamilton on drums, Red Mack on trumpet and Joe Comfort on a jug!

The Daily Variety said of *You'll Never Get Rich* 'Columbia steps into the big time musical field with *You'll Never Get Rich*, a happy combination of music, dancing and comedy that spells box office. The teaming of Fred Astaire and Rita Hayworth is also another happy combination. The picture ranks easily with Astaire's best and displays another side of Miss Hayworth's talents, a side that will find much favour. Her work will stand up to any comparison.'

And indeed it did. Fred's usual elegance and charm, not diminished by the fact that he spent much of the picture in army uniform, surmounted the age gap between him and Rita, and Rita herself certainly had one big plus over Ginger Rogers. She actually looked as though she was enjoying herself. Ginger, although she danced beautifully and smiled a lot during all those numbers at RKO sometimes gave the impression that the smile was a trifle fixed and that, on occasion, she was under a certain amount of strain. Rita, however, enjoyed it all immensely. She had grace and verve and there was an excitement about her. She had an instinctive sense of rhythm and her precision was uncanny.

Before Fred and Rita could get together for the second of their two films, however, Fred had another commitment to Paramount to appear in a movie called *Holiday Inn* (1942). The prospect of returning to the Paramount stages must have seemed a little daunting after the experience of *Second Chorus* but this time there were special attractions. One was that the score of the musical

was being written by his old buddy Irving Berlin, the other was that his co-star was to be Bing Crosby.

The resulting movie was a pleasant little entertainment revolving around a couple of song and dance men who split up when one of them turns a New England farm into a nightclub which opens only on holidays. As usual the plot mattered little, the music a lot. And there was plenty of it in *Holiday Inn*. Bing sang no fewer than nine times including the Oscar winning 'White Christmas' and a duet with Fred to 'I'll Capture Your Heart Singing' and Fred took to the floor on six occasions. He was at his best in a cleverly staged trick dance involving fire-crackers and a dance in which he is 'drunk' but somehow gets through to the end with his partner.

Holiday Inn also reunited Fred with his former RKO colleague director Mark Sandrich so it was something of a reunion picture all round. It opened in New York in August 1942.

Just two months earlier Fred received one of the best presents of his life – a baby daughter, Ava, presented to him by an equally delighted Phyllis. There were many in Hollywood who cast envious

Bubbles and foam everywhere! Fred and Lucille Bremer filming the much mutilated 'There's Beauty Everywhere' sequence in the grand finale of Ziegfeld Follies *(MGM, 1945).*

Opposite: 'Limehouse
Blues'. Fred with Lucille
Bremer. Director
Minnelli's flair for colour
is perfectly demonstrated
with this shot from
Ziegfeld Follies
(MGM, 1945).

Left: 'Limehouse Blues'.
An almost unrecognisable
Fred as the victim of
Oriental harlot Lucille
Bremer in one of the more
successful musical episodes
in MGM's 1945
extravaganza Ziegfeld
Follies.

eyes at the marriage and family of the Astaires. In Hollywood a happy and private union such as theirs was not thought to be possible. Fred and Phyllis continually proved them wrong as the years went by.

The title of Fred's second Columbia movie, *You Were Never Lovelier* (1942), might well have been dedicated to the newly arrived Ava. Harry Cohn however, had Rita Hayworth in mind, and rightly so for she had now assumed the title of 'love goddess' and was just about the most beautiful woman around in Hollywood.

For the new picture Cohn brought in Jerome

Kern to write the music and Johnny Mercer to conjure up the lyrics. Both said yes without a second thought even though it meant working at a small studio and not at one of the giants. No doubt Fred's name had much to do with their acceptance of the assignment but there was no denying the fact that when Harry Cohn wanted something he invariably got it. He was never mean with money but, even though he couldn't match the fees of the larger studios, people still didn't seem to be able to say no to him. He always got the talent when he wanted it.

At one stage there was talk of making *You Were*

Never Lovelier in colour. But with America now in the war after Pearl Harbor and the overseas European markets rapidly diminishing it was decided to hold back for just a little longer on Columbia's first colour feature.

As it turned out, *You Were Never Lovelier* didn't need colour. It was a smash. If *You'll Never Get Rich* had been the hors-d'oeuvre the second movie was very definitely the main meal. The setting was Buenos Aires and the story had Fred as a horse-playing nightclub dancer from New York romancing the beautiful but aloof Rita, the second of four daughters of nightclub owner Adolphe Menjou. Lyricist Johnny Mercer summed it up as being one of those nice pictures: 'It was a kind of dressy film: Fred was always in tails going through french windows, dancing on the terrace, one of those pictures.'

Indeed it was 'one of those pictures'. In fact, it was the closest Fred had come to reaching the standard of an RKO movie since he had left that studio. *Time* magazine hailed Rita as the best partner he'd ever had. And they meshed together perfectly. In the Harlem globetrot, 'The Shorty

George', they set the screen alight and in the final number 'I'm Old-fashioned' they provided one of the finest sequences in any musical film from any Hollywood studio. Fred dances with Rita first on a moonlit terrace, then in a garden. The steps change from old-fashioned to Latin American and then merge into some ecstatically fast whirls as Fred, with inimitable deftness and speed, waltzes Rita off into the end titles. It was magic time once again.

Fred worked Rita hard on *You Were Never Lovelier*. She said later: 'Dancing is hard work whether you're dancing with Fred Astaire or Gene Kelly or anybody else. You have to be fit and you have to be able to love it.'

The wife of the film's director William Seiter recalled that Fred worked so hard on the film that he lost 20 pounds in weight. During the filming of 'The Shorty George' number Rita became so enthusiastic about things that she tripped, struck her chin on the floor and was knocked out. Fred almost fainted when he saw her stretched out on the floor.

At Columbia Fred had a difficult time finding suitable out-of-the-way locations in which to rehearse his dances with Rita. One he did find was a funeral parlour of the nearby Hollywood Cemetery, which Columbia rented. The only problem was that every time a funeral procession came through the cemetery gates, rehearsals had to be halted until the service was over and the mourners had departed.

In his autobiography *Steps In Time*, Fred wrote: 'We pulled some good dance material out of those weird surroundings. Rita and I had a good time with 'The Shorty George' number which did not originate in the funeral parlour but was devised on Sundays at the studio when we had the place to ourselves.'

Another top number in the film was the delightful 'Dearly Beloved', danced by Fred and Rita and sung by Nan Wynn who dubbed for Rita throughout the movie's musical numbers. In fact, whereas in the previous Astaire/Hayworth film Cole Porter had delivered one of his few mediocre scores, Jerome Kern came through things with flying colours on *You Were Never Lovelier*. Except when he was asked to write a song for the Xavier Cugat Band. 'I don't write Spanish songs,' he told Harry Cohn. 'I don't write anything unless I can write it well, and I can't write Spanish songs.'

Fred didn't reserve his singing and dancing for the screen in 1942. Like other top stars he made strenuous efforts to sell war bonds. Fred's brief was to dance a number, then sing a number, then ask those in the audience to purchase war bonds for America. He travelled from one end of the country to the other, performing not only in theatres and cinemas but also at celebrity banquets, service bases and just about anywhere where there was a chance of raising the much needed money. It was exhausting work and he never let up. Fred was always a hard taskmaster and never more so than on himself. His biggest triumph came at Madison Square Garden where $86 million was raised in one night.

Studios, of course, kept pressing him for movies. When his deal with Columbia came to an end he received an invitation to return to RKO who had fallen on lean times in the early 1940s and were once again finding it difficult to make ends meet. Their idea was to try to tempt Fred and Ginger back for another blockbuster. The idea didn't work out. They got Fred but they didn't get Ginger. And instead of Ginger, Fred got Joan Leslie who had just enjoyed a hit with James Cagney in *Yankee Doodle Dandy*.

The picture they made together was *The Sky's The Limit* (1943). Fred played an American flier in the Flying Tiger Squadron who opts out of a coast-to-coast glory tour and plumps instead for a trip to New York where he meets and falls for Joan Leslie. It was a mediocre effort. The most memorable things about the picture were that, for the first time, Fred was not called on to appear at least once in white tie and tails and that he introduced the Johnny Mercer/Harold Arlen standard 'One For My Baby'.

By 1944 Fred was determined to make a trip to Europe to entertain the troops. Apart from his pictures at Columbia he felt that he had not made any great contribution to the screen musical since his days at RKO in the 1930s and that he would be better off employed dancing 'live' for the GIs in Europe. He had just one more commitment to fulfil before he could make the trip. He had to star in an MGM extravaganza called *Ziegfeld Follies* (1945).

The movie was a revue-type musical that was to be strung together (initially by George Sidney but eventually by Vincente Minnelli) and involve just about every major star on the MGM lot. It wasn't one of Arthur Freed's brightest ideas but, if nothing else, it had variety and was presided over by William Powell as the long-dead Ziegfeld who looks down from heaven and smiles benevolently as the Metro stars (among them Judy Garland, Esther Williams, Lucille Ball, Kathryn Grayson and Red Skelton) go through one musical and comedy number after another.

MGM's problem was that they rather overdid things. When it came to previewing the film at Hollywood's Westwood Theatre there were some 18 numbers and sketches in the film. Fred appeared in 6, more than any other star. When those in the preview audience rose to their feet and collectively began rubbing the backs of their numb legs they found they had been sitting watching the screen for 2 hours and 53 minutes.

Not surprisingly, the reaction at the preview was decidedly on the cool side and, as was the case in those days, MGM took the sneak preview very seriously. The word went out from Mayer and Freed: 'Cut!' And that inevitably meant that just about everyone connected with the film tried to have their say as to what should or should not go. At one stage Roger Edens commented wryly: 'If they go on like this we can always release it as a short with one number.' He didn't indicate what title he might use but presumably *Ziegfeld's Folly* might have been appropriate.

The upshot of all the bickering was that two sketches in which Jimmy Durante appeared were cut, as was the 'Baby Snooks' routine of Fanny Brice. Esther Williams was trimmed above the waterline but left intact underwater, a western number sung by operatic tenor James Melton was snipped and so too was the song 'Liza' in which Avon Long sang to Lena Horne and ten dancers. Fred was also a casualty. His 'If Swing Goes I Go Too' (a number Fred had never liked) disappeared as did his participation in a lavish and extravagant opus called 'There's Beauty Everywhere' which involved a huge ascending set and thousands of bubbles.

In view of all the problems they encountered filming the number, Fred and the others were probably more than a little annoyed that most of their scenes finished up on the cutting-room floor. The bubbles were the trouble. They simply got out of control. They were meant first to obscure then

Overleaf: *Fred and Gene Kelly teamed together at MGM in the all-star revue* Ziegfeld Follies. *The number: 'The Babbitt And The Bromide'*.

Opposite: *Fred and Gene Kelly in 'The Babbitt And The Bromide' from* Ziegfeld Follies *(MGM, 1945).*

Left: *Fred behind the camera with director Vincente Minnelli during the filming of his 1945 musical* Yolanda And The Thief *(MGM).*

reveal each changing image in the musical sequence and act as a kind of substitute for the cinematic dissolve (fading one scene into another). All they actually succeeded in doing was choking cast and crew half to death.

The bubbles were pumped on to the set by a group of prop men and special effects geniuses who between them fed a soap bubble machine with aerosol and injected it with air and hot water. The result was that the bubbles kept floating to the top of the set and bursting. And once they burst they emitted a noxious gas that was so overpowering that Minnelli, who was on the camera boom, high up with his cameraman Charles Rosher, had to cling on for dear life as Rosher fainted from the fumes and both of them had to be lowered 40 feet to the floor.

The scene was almost like that in a Hal Roach comedy with bubbles streaming down the studio walls and into every crevice. Studio 'grips' (or general handymen), all of them strategically placed to control the bubbles, tried valiantly to swat the ones that wouldn't behave. All told it took 7 days to film the fiasco. On one of those days Fred arrived with a temperature of 102 having just been injected 5 times for his impending United Services Organisation (USO) trip to Europe. He felt ill and he felt miserable. To plunge with Lucille Bremer into the bubbles simply added to his misery. Eyes streamed and became red raw and the coughing became almost unstoppable. It seemed as though the filming of the number would never

end. But thankfully it did.

In the final version of the film only Kathryn Grayson and the Ziegfeld girls remain.

Still, Fred came out of things as well as anybody in *Ziegfeld Follies*, probably more so. His rendering of 'Limehouse Blues', shot on the set left over from *The Picture Of Dorian Gray*, is a masterpiece of subtlety and artistic timing. Fred, black-suited, black-hatted and almost unrecognisable as a slant-eyed, sad-mouthed Chinaman, brings a pathos to his balletic routines which end with his death and a vision of unfulfilled love for a Chinese girl.

He was at his best too in the Arthur Freed/ Harry Warren number 'This Heart Of Mine' in which he featured as a dapper jewel thief who crashes an elegant party and makes a play for the ravishing Lucille Bremer. His number with Gene Kelly, 'The Babbitt And The Bromide', an old Gershwin nonsense song which he had first danced to with Adele in *Funny Face*, was hardly in the same class but it did at least mark the only occasion when Fred and Gene danced together on screen, apart from the rather tentative steps they took together some 30 years later when acting as co-hosts for *That's Entertainment Part II*.

Kelly doesn't remember the number with any great affection ('I thought I looked like a klotz,' he recalled later) and would much rather have done 'Pass That Peace Pipe' which had been specially written for the film by Roger Edens, Hugh Martin and Ralph Blane but which wasn't thought good enough to use. The number was eventually

Opposite: *Fred and Lucille Bremer perform a 'dream ballet' in MGM's* Yolanda And The Thief. *The sequence lasted for 16 minutes on screen.*

Right: *Fred as a charming thief and Lucille Bremer as the wealthy heiress he tries to con. A scene from the 1945 musical* Yolanda And The Thief *(MGM).*

included in *Good News* two years later and was nominated for an Academy Award!

'The Babbitt And The Bromide' tells of two men who meet on a street, say hello and go through an ordinary everyday conversation. Ten years later they meet again and go through the same routine. The routine carries on in the same manner until they meet for the last time in heaven and go through the motions yet again, this time with harps.

'The thing I remember most plainly about "The Babbitt And The Bromide"', says Kelly, 'was the rehearsals. Fred was the senior partner and if I felt there was any conflict or any doubt about any step I would certainly defer to him, but he made it so there wasn't any. There wasn't a gentler or nicer man I ever worked with. That isn't to say Fred isn't a very tough worker. He can be as hard as nails, and I've seen him be that way, but he's only that way because he wants his dances as well as can be. Fred felt good about the number because he had done it before, in a show together with his sister Adele.'

Fred left for Europe as soon as his scenes in *Ziegfeld Follies* had been completed. He wore a uniform but no badge of rank and, like his fellow entertainers in the USO, became known as one of the 'soldiers in greasepaint'.

He was received rapturously wherever he went. Soldiers everywhere, first in London, later in Europe after the D-day invasions had begun, clamoured to see him perform. And perform he did in just about any setting he could find. Sometimes he would perform for audiences of just 200, sometimes for those of 2000 or more.

For Fred the back of a truck would do. Or a makeshift platform. If he visited an army hospital he would spring from empty bed to empty bed. In a barracks he would use just a table or even a chair. If the room was empty of furniture he would just dance. Those who remember Fred's impromptu performances in Europe during the early days of the invasion have never forgotten them. Many a GI had his day brightened by Fred's singing and dancing. And just as on his movies Fred didn't

Opposite: 'A Couple Of Song And Dance Men'. Fred and Bing Crosby in one of the highlights of Blue Skies (Paramount, 1946).

Right: 'What Have I Got Myself Into?' Fred seems to be saying to Frank Morgan in this scene from Yolanda And The Thief (MGM). The film was a critical success but failed at the box office.

spare himself. He often performed three or four times a day, travelling hundreds of miles from one 'entertainment stop' to another.

The one black spot during Fred's overseas tour was the news of the death of Adele's husband Charles. He had been ill for some time and his was a sad, lonely death. He was nursed by his mother during his last days because Adele, who was hundreds of miles away working for the American Red Cross, couldn't get a permit to cross the Irish Sea to Lismore as it was just before D-day. All in all Adele's life had been plagued with ill-fortune since she had retired from show business but at least she and Fred managed to get together for a night at Rainbow Corner, the social centre of London's Shaftesbury Avenue where soldiers gathered every day before preparing themselves for the horrors they were to encounter overseas.

Fred was many months in Europe. He met up with many fellow entertainers, among them his old starring partner of *Holiday Inn*, Bing Crosby, and when he returned at last to the States on the *Queen Mary* (he and Bing did regular nightly shows for the troops on board) he was, even for him, exhausted. When he arrived back at his home on Summit Drive he told Phyllis that all he wanted was a bit of peace and quiet and the chance to relax. His son was now eight years old and informed him that he didn't think he'd be following in his father's footsteps. Fred didn't mind. In fact, he was very doubtful whether he'd be following in his own footsteps. Doctors had warned him that every time he danced, especially the *way* he danced, he would tax his heart.

Phyllis, who by now had become so used to Fred's dithering about retirement, took a 'I'll believe it when I see it attitude' and calmly let Fred ponder the future and recharge the batteries.

But once those batteries were recharged it was the same old story as before. Fred thought he might just have one final fling at the movies, just to see if he could come up with something a little different with his dance routines. It was the decision Phyllis had expected.

MGM was obviously the studio to concentrate on (the bubble machine was no longer in use for musicals!) so once again he headed in the direction of Culver City. The film that drew him there was *Yolanda And The Thief* (1945), a kind of reworking and expanded version of the 'This Heart Is Mine' number from *Ziegfeld Follies*. Another plus as far as Fred was concerned was that it was to be directed by Vincente Minnelli who was then fast rising to become the major director at Metro.

The story was set in a mythical South American country called Patria or, as Fred describes it in the film, 'a cemetery with a train running through it!' Fred plays a crooked gambler who pretends to be the supernaturally materialised guardian angel of a beautiful and extremely gullible young heiress and then tries to swindle her out of her fortune.

The film opened at the Capitol Theatre, New York, where it received a rave notice from Bosley Crowther in *The New York Times*: 'Elegance is the quality with which the producers have endowed this singing and dancing rendition of a sophisticated fairy tale. For brilliance and colour of the settings and costumes are nigh beyond compare –

as rich and theatrically tasteful as any we've ever seen. The ensemble numbers are presented by Mr Minnelli with remarkable grace. And the terpsichorean cavorting of Lucille Bremer and Fred Astaire is simply grand. A dream ballet number, expanded against Daliesque décor with Mr Astaire as the dreamer is a thing of pictorial delight. And a rhythm dance, done to the melody of Mr Freed's "Coffee Time", puts movement and colour to such uses as you seldom behold on the screen.'

Crowther did admit that the story, such as it was, was laboured and flat, and a bit hard going but ended his notice by stating: 'The visual felicities and the wackiness of the main idea hold the show together and make it something most profitable to see.'

The film, however, was not profitable in any other sense. The public stayed away in droves. A fantasy in a never-never land was not what audiences who had been through a hideous war wanted to see late in 1945. Realism, not sophistication, was what they wanted, even in a musical. And they rejected *Yolanda And The Thief* out of hand. The film flopped badly. Admittedly it was something of an experiment but it also indicated that even the multi-talented Arthur Freed unit could miscalculate. Sophistication worked and found a ready audience on Broadway but not in the cinema. Arthur Freed would dabble again in the ultra-sophisticated musical when he filmed *The Pirate* (this time with Gene Kelly) in 1948 but when that also flopped he opted for keeping his musicals, inventive as they were, with their feet on the ground.

The financial failure of *Yolanda And The Thief* disappointed Fred. He had felt the film was a little out of the normal run and might find an audience. The fact that it didn't find any kind of an audience caused him to wonder whether he now had any place in the postwar cinema. Also whether his own style of dancing was out of date.

MGM tried to tempt him with a remake of the turn-of-the-century Broadway hit *The Belle Of New York*, but even though Freed commissioned Harry Warren and Johnny Mercer to write new songs, Fred remained only lukewarm.

His spirits lifted somewhat when he got an urgent telephone call from his old chum Bing Crosby. Bing was at Paramount filming a musical called *Blue Skies* (1946). And he was in trouble. His problem was that he wasn't getting on very well with his co-star Paul Draper, a top Broadway performer who was having some difficulty in coming to terms with Hollywood and coping with a slight stammer that wasn't exactly helping him in his romantic scenes with Joan Caulfield. Nor was he really hitting it off with producer-director Mark Sandrich. Bing told Fred that he felt that it wouldn't be too long before Draper was off the picture and would he consider replacing him.

The combination of Mark Sandrich and Irving Berlin (there were some 30 Berlin numbers featured in the movie) proved irresistible to Fred. He told Bing that if the worst happened to get in

touch. Unfortunately the worst did happen but in a different sense. Mark Sandrich was struck down by a heart attack and died at the early age of 45. A new producer, Sol Siegel, and director, Stuart Heisler, were brought in to carry on with the picture. Draper found himself getting on even less well with the replacements than he had done with Sandrich and the result was that he was replaced. The door was open for Fred and he joined the company, saddened at the loss of his friend Mark Sandrich but happy to be working again with Hermes Pan who was dance director on the picture.

Before he began work on *Blue Skies*, however, Fred let it be known that he had now definitely made up his mind to retire. He was 47, his peak years (or what he thought were his peak years) were behind him and after *Blue Skies* it would be a happy contented life of retirement.

Blue Skies was really nothing more than a piece of musical nonsense, a peg on which to hang a series of Berlin numbers, some old, some new. It centred on a couple of song and dance men who vie for the affections of the same girl. Bing gets her, Fred doesn't. Whenever the romance fell flat or the music stopped (which wasn't often) Billy DeWolfe was around to mug up some comedy. It was, as they say in the trade, a bit of a mishmash.

But just occasionally it reached level A when for most of the time it had been floundering around on levels C and D and even below. One such highspot was when Fred and Bing joined forces for 'A Couple Of Song And Dance Men'. But *the* highspot was when Fred once more donned top hat, white tie and tails and executed the four-minute number 'Puttin' On The Ritz'.

The number takes the breath away with its sheer virtuosity. It opens with Fred alone in a smartly furnished room and with only a cane for a prop. As he breaks into the refrain 'Have you seen the well-to-do up and down Park Avenue' he first flirts with the cane, cajoles it, seduces it, jumps across it and dances round it and smacks it time and again into the marble floor as he goes into one breathtaking routine after another. In the last minute of the song he comes face to face with a group of similarly dressed Astaires and taps the dance out into a furious climax.

Said Bosley Crowther in *The New York Times*: 'Turned out in striped pants and top hat, Mr A makes his educated feet talk a persuasive language that is thrilling to conjugate. The number ends with some process screen trickery in which a dozen or so midget Astaires back up the tapping soloist in a beautiful surge of clickety-clicks. If this film is Mr A's swan song, as he has heartlessly announced it will be, then he has climaxed his many years of hoofing with a properly superlative "must-see".'

For many people, 'Puttin' On The Ritz' was and still is the best Fred Astaire number ever put on screen. As Fred had intended it should be. If he was going out of movies at the age of 47, he was determined to go out in style.

Irving Berlin's 'Puttin'
On The Ritz', the
number that was supposed
to bring Fred's career to
a close in Blue Skies in
1946 (Paramount).

SHAKIN' THE BLUES AWAY

Fred never actually referred to his retirement from the screen as such. He preferred to call it 'a temporary leave of absence' or 'a mental retirement'. On other occasions he would say that he was simply resting from creating new steps and ideas for dance numbers.

The hobby that most occupied him in the months following the completion of *Blue Skies* was horses. Or rather, horse. The horse in question was called Triplicate which sounds almost as though it may have been a number from one of Fred's films but was, in fact, the name of a colt Fred had bought as a three-year-old for $6000.

Fred had always enjoyed himself at the races. In 1946 he enjoyed himself even more for it turned out that he was no mean judge of horse flesh. Triplicate turned out to be a winner. He won the San Juan Capistrano Handicap at Santa Anita and followed that by romping home in the Gold Cup at Hollywood Park, earning Fred over $80,000 in prize-money, plus $6000 which Fred won by placing a small wager on him. He won yet again in the Golden Gate Handicap in San Francisco and, in all, amassed $240,000 before ankle trouble in 1948 ended his career and he was put out to stud in Kentucky.

Fred also interested himself in dancing schools. He had noted that the Arthur Murray School of Dancing had been doing big business and decided to cash in on the trend. In 1947 he opened his first dancing school on New York's elegant Park Avenue and then followed with others in Kansas, Los Angeles, San Francisco and London. Yet more followed and Fred found himself a successful businessman as well as a star name.

Business, however, wasn't exactly Fred's scene. He was pleased the schools were succeeding but his interest in them was no more than cursory. The trouble was he didn't feel as though he was old enough to settle down. Forty-seven going on 48 was not really the age at which to retire from anything, especially movies. Most actors went on into their 70s, some into their 80s and beyond. Admittedly dancing was different and demanded more physical fitness but even so, 47/48 *was* still a bit on the young side.

Fred's main problem was that he had no motivation. He had a lovely Hollywood home on Summit Drive, a new ranch, a perfect family, just about everything a man could want. He was under no pressure, he had no financial worries, he didn't have to be at the studio every morning and he could play a relaxing round of golf whenever he so desired. Almost Utopia, in fact. Indeed, it would have been for many men. But not Fred. The opening lyrics of a famous song read 'After You Get What You Want You Don't Want It'. It wasn't *quite* that with Fred but the sentiments of the song weren't too wide of the mark. Creating something out of nothing had always been the key for Fred. Now he was creating nothing.

To keep his hand, or rather his feet in, he danced daily inside his house to music on a record player, practising new steps and new routines and keeping himself not only physically fit but also mentally alert. Later in his career he was to comment: 'Dancing is approximately 80 per cent brainwork, only 20 per cent of the strain is on the feet.'

The strain was certainly on poor Gene Kelly's feet one Saturday morning in October 1947. He was playing a game of touch football in the grounds of his Hollywood home and becoming deeply involved in the game when he tripped and fell full stretch. A couple of players tumbled on top

of him. One of them stabbed his foot against Gene's ankle. There's no record of Gene's exact words then, but, if there was, they would probably be unprintable. The net result was that he couldn't get up. And when he *was* pulled gingerly to his feet he found he couldn't stand. The game of football had produced a broken ankle.

Bad enough for any dancer, of course, but when you had been rehearsing for a month with Judy Garland for a brand new MGM musical called *Easter Parade*, just about disastrous. The doctors told Gene that the ankle would mend but that it would take weeks, possibly months to get it back into shape. Gene would have to be patient. Gene, in fact, had no option.

Not so producer Arthur Freed at MGM. He *had* to have an option. When Gene rang with the news he slumped back in his chair as though the sky had fallen in. And in some ways it had. In those days studios such as MGM ran like clockwork. Films that were being shot one year were already booked into New York openings for the next. And *Easter Parade* was no exception. It was down to open in New York in June the following year, 1948.

Freed knew there was no way he could halt production. It would have been too costly. The only alternative was a replacement. To replace

Above: *Fred providing a few impromptu steps for the personally trained dance instructors who operated his post-war dance schools.*

Opposite: *Fred, pictured at his Hollywood home after 'ending' his film career in* Blue Skies.

THE HAPPIEST MUSICAL EVER MADE IS

Irving Berlin's

EASTER PARADE

COLOR BY TECHNICOLOR from M·G·M

Hear ♪♪ 17 OF IRVING BERLIN'S GREATEST SONGS . . . including such hits as "EASTER PARADE" · "STEPPIN' OUT WITH MY BABY" · "IT ONLY HAPPENS WHEN I DANCE WITH YOU" · "BETTER LUCK NEXT TIME" · "A FELLA WITH AN UMBRELLA" · "A COUPLE OF SWELLS" (Available on M·G·M Records)

Starring JUDY GARLAND · FRED ASTAIRE

PETER LAWFORD · ANN MILLER

SCREEN PLAY BY SIDNEY SHELDON, FRANCES GOODRICH and ALBERT HACKETT · ORIGINAL STORY BY FRANCES GOODRICH and ALBERT HACKETT · A METRO-GOLDWYN-MAYER PICTURE

Lyrics and Music by IRVING BERLIN · Musical Numbers Directed by ROBERT ALTON · Directed by CHARLES WALTERS · Produced by ARTHUR FREED

The MGM advertisement announcing Fred's comeback picture Easter Parade, *an Oscar winner in 1948 for the best scoring of a musical.*

Gene Kelly however was no easy matter. Since Fred's retirement Gene had established himself as the most creative screen hoofer and there weren't many like him around. Generally speaking a studio could replace an actor or actress within half an hour from its own gallery of stars. That's why they had such a large contingent of contract players. In fact one such star, Cyd Charisse, had already been replaced by Ann Miller on *Easter Parade*.

It was Arthur Freed who thought of Fred. With Gene's blessing, he rang and explained the situation. Fred told him that he was flattered to be asked but that he wasn't really in the movie market any more. Freed persisted. Fred hesitated. He told Freed that he'd think about it but that he would have to check with Gene first.

He rang Gene and said: 'Look, I don't want to do this. Why don't you wait and then do it?' Waiting of course was impossible. Gene gave him the go-ahead. He later said: 'Whatever blessing I

was empowered to give him, I gave.'

So it was that in November 1947 Fred went back before the cameras at Culver City. He didn't know it then but as he passed through the entrance of that great studio he was about to start the final phase of his career. What neither he nor anyone else realised was that that final phase was to last for something like another 35 years!

Easter Parade was a movie of great charm but, true to form, it had a story of very little consequence. It was set in the gentler, far off days of 1912, a period which composer Irving Berlin (for it was he again who was writing the score) remembered with great affection. Fred played one half of a dancing partnership who gets stranded when the other half, Ann Miller, decides to go solo. Fred looks for someone else, finds her in the chorus of a small nightclub and then gradually turns her into a dancing star alongside him. It was a kind of *Pygmalion* story with Technicolor plus MGM sets.

To all intents and purposes, it was just another musical on the MGM schedule, a good one admittedly and one with a large budget, but just another musical. But it certainly didn't feel like another musical when Fred first did a few taps on the MGM rehearsal stages. With his arrival the film acquired some tension. It had become Fred's 'come-back' picture which meant, of course, that it got more publicity than any other film then shooting on the MGM lot. It was also a test movie for Judy Garland who not long before had allegedly smashed a bathroom mirror and made an attempt at suicide by cutting her wrists with broken glass. She had been under psychiatric care for some time and was in a very fragile condition.

Judy's psychiatrist had told studio boss Louis B. Mayer that she would be OK for work but that it might be better if Vincente Minnelli who was then her husband and who had originally been set to direct the picture remained as just her husband and not her director at work. The strain, he felt, might be too much.

Arthur Freed reluctantly told Minnelli that he would have to stand down. He hired in his stead Charles Walters, a former choreographer/dance director who had just made a hit with the college musical *Good News*. Walters was astonished. He didn't know why he had been chosen. He had heard rumours. But that didn't matter. With only his second movie he was going to direct Fred Astaire and Judy Garland in their first film together.

He realised of course that Judy was not a person to be fooled with. He came on to the picture just five days after Fred and Judy had been rehearsing together. He later remembered: 'Judy loved to growl, loved to pretend. She turned to me and said "Look sweetie, I'm no June Allyson you know. Don't get cute with me. None of that batting the eyelids bit or fluffing the hair routine for me, buddy. I'm Judy Garland and just you watch it!"'

And Chuck Walters did watch it, very care-

Easter Parade *(MGM, 1948). Fred with Ann Miller.*

fully. But he liked Judy and she liked him. And they struck up something of a rapport between them. What's more Judy worked well with Fred. She rehearsed seriously and picked up complicated dance routines quickly.

She certainly needed to for there were some 20 Irving Berlin numbers in *Easter Parade*. Berlin had been contracted to write eight new numbers for the movie but once he'd completed the assignment he was approached by Arthur Freed with a suggestion for an extra song. Freed felt there should be a comedy number in the movie, one specially written for the two stars. Berlin agreed to write it, even though he'd completed his eight songs. He came up with one called 'Let's Take An Old-Fashioned Walk'. He played it for Freed, waiting for his reaction. Freed shook his head. 'I don't care for it, Irving,' he said apologetically. Berlin, always a man to take things in his stride, said: 'OK. Forget about it. I can always use it some-

where else.' An hour later he returned to Arthur Freed's office, this time with 'A Couple Of Swells' which became the most popular song of the picture with Fred and Judy singing and dancing in tramp costume.

The public and the critics loved *Easter Parade*. They enjoyed seeing Fred back in action, especially when he was in such devastating form with his trick number, the 'Drum Crazy' routine. Another high spot was his 'Steppin' Out With My Baby' in which he danced in turn with three beautiful partners in three different moods of dance – a modified ballet, a sultry blues number and a lively jitterbug – before changing the pace yet again and swinging into a solo tap dance that reaches its climax in slow motion.

The public also enjoyed Fred and Judy together, the music (as well they should for it ranks as one of Berlin's finest scores) and just about everything in the picture. And 'everything' included Ann

112

Miller who in one number sent the temperature rising with 'Shakin' The Blues Away'.

It seemed as though Fred had never been away. The critic of *The New York Times* spoke for many when he wrote of the film: 'Fred Astaire, who has no peer, is dancing at the top of his form and let's hope that he'll never again talk about retiring as he did after *Blue Skies*. Maybe Mr Astaire has turned his feet to more intricate steps in previous pictures, but for sheer simplicity and poetry of motion his dancing in *Easter Parade* would be difficult to equal, much less better. In solo and in tandem with either Miss Garland or Miss Miller the incomparable Astaire glides effortlessly through numerous routines. His opening number dancing out an Easter shopping mission for his sweetheart, is gay and debonair and involves an intriguing contest with a small boy in a toy shop over the possession of the last remaining stuffed bunny.'

Gene Kelly, but for whom Fred might have stayed forever in retirement, was delighted that Fred had at last joined the Freed troupe. He said later that he was pleased to be responsible for getting Fred back but that every time he saw the scene in which Fred and Judy sang 'A Couple Of

Swells' he got a twinge of regret.

Easter Parade came in under budget, something of an achievement for a Garland movie, at a cost of $2½ million. On its first release it grossed nearly $7 million, a very healthy profit indeed. Little wonder that MGM were pleased that Fred had returned to the screen and little wonder also that they immediately set about casting him and Judy in another musical together. *Easter Parade* had been a happy experience all round and now that Fred had decided to become a permanent member of the Arthur Freed line-up the studio had just about the ideal musical set-up.

Fred was perfectly happy. Any doubts he may have had about accepting the *Easter Parade* assignment were now long past. He was back and as far as he was concerned retirement was a word that he never considered again.

The new movie was announced as *You Made Me Love You*. Chuck Walters was again named as director and Betty Comden and Adolph Green were given the job of conjuring up a story to accompany the music of Harry Warren and lyrics of Ira Gershwin. They came up with a tale of a Broadway dancing team who are always bickering

and who split up when the female half decides that she would like to have a crack at becoming a dramatic actress. After the usual ups and downs and a number of comic interludes from the wisecracking Oscar Levant they come together again.

Hardly original material but, with Harry Warren and Ira Gershwin in charge of the musical side of things, story originality was hardly the most important part of the movie.

The first indication that *The Barkleys Of Broadway* (1949) (as *You Made Me Love You* was eventually renamed) was not going to be as enjoyable or as easy-going an experience as *Easter Parade* came when Judy Garland first attended rehearsals in June 1948. There were many who had hoped that the success of her partnership with Fred would help stabilise her and start her career off on another, even more successful, phase. But the hopes were soon dashed. During the second week of rehearsals she began to falter. By the third week she was coming in late, sometimes not turning up at all. Her mental problems had started up all over again. She suffered heavy depressions and she also had weight problems.

Very soon there was a crisis. Freed conferred with Louis B. Mayer. They contacted Judy's personal physician, Dr Schelman. He said if Judy continued on the film it would be a risky business for all concerned. Judy, he told Freed, could conceivably work for four or five days but only under medication. After that might come some bad days when she would not be able to work at all and then another five-day work period. And so on.

It was obviously a risk that MGM could not afford to take. *The Barkleys Of Broadway* was a high budget musical. A replacement was again the only solution. Judy was duly taken off the picture. That in itself came as no great surprise to anyone in the industry or outside it. What did come as a surprise was the name of Judy's replacement – Ginger Rogers!

Just how Arthur Freed came up with Ginger's name after so many years has always remained something of a mystery. One possible answer was that after the premiere of *Easter Parade* Ginger had sent Freed a telegram congratulating him on the picture and saying how much she had enjoyed it. And that may have stuck in the back of Freed's mind. But whatever the reason, Ginger it was. This both pleased and dismayed Fred. He was sorry about Judy for he had enjoyed working with her on *Easter Parade* and was genuinely fond of her. On the other hand he was pleased to be back with Ginger after an absence of ten years – and this time the film was to be in colour.

The change of plans didn't entirely please the two composers for there was a marked difference between Judy and Ginger as performers and a song that might suit Judy would not do at all for Ginger. Consequently a song called 'Natchez On The Mississippi' was dropped. As was a hillbilly number called 'The Courtship of Elmer And Ella'

and a comic ballet called 'Poetry In Motion'.

Charles Walters, who had already had the thrill of directing Astaire and Garland in a movie, now had the unexpected pleasure of directing Fred and Ginger in their come-back picture but it didn't quite turn out as he had expected. 'I'll never forget that day,' he later recalled. 'Fred was rehearsing the "Shoes With Wings On" number in a theatre set and Ginger came down the aisle, walked up on to the stage and embraced with Fred. I started to cry. I just broke down. I thought I just can't believe that I will be directing Astaire and Rogers. It was quite a thrill. But quite a shock to find out that Mr Astaire is not too keen about Miss Rogers. And I'm still trying to find out why. With the success and the money the two of them made how could he not like Ginger Rogers?'

Walters himself offered his own explanation: 'You know what it boils down to? She's too big. It's that simple. She's too big. Too tall.'

On the other hand Chuck Walters may well have been wrong in his assumption especially as Ginger made a joke about her height when she started rehearsing with Fred for the picture. Fred himself remembered it well: 'When we finally got round to shooting our first dance I thought for some reason that Ginger seemed taller than usual. I

Above: *Fred, about to become 'Drum Crazy' in a toy store in his celebrated solo routine in* Easter Parade *(MGM, 1948).*

Opposite: *Still one of the most popular numbers in any MGM musical, 'A Couple Of Swells', performed by Fred and Judy Garland in tramp costume in* Easter Parade *(MGM, 1948).*

asked Hermes Pan, "Am I crazy or is Ginger on stilts?" He said, "I know something is different." I went to Ginger and said "Hey, have you grown or have I shrunk?" She laughed and confessed she had sneaked some high heels over on me.'

Musically, *The Barkleys Of Broadway* is an inferior picture to *Easter Parade*. The two piano interludes of Oscar Levant, the first to 'The Sabre Dance', the second a three-minute version of Tchaikovsky's First Piano Concerto, simply hold up the action, good though they are, and such songs as 'My One And Only Highland Fling', a kind of Scottish 'Couple Of Swells' performed by Fred and Ginger and 'You'd Be So Hard To Replace', a serenade by Fred to Ginger are instantly forgettable.

But there are compensations. The rehearsal tap routine 'Bouncin' The Blues' proved that the pair had lost none of their old magic as did a reprise, shot against beautiful MGM drapes constantly changing colour from mauve to green to orange, of 'They Can't Take That Away From Me' the number Fred and Ginger had first performed 12 years earlier in *Shall We Dance?*

Best of all was Fred's solo 'Shoes With Wings On', arguably his most inventive solo routine at MGM. Dance director Hermes Pan got the idea for the number from *The Sorcerer's Apprentice*. During rehearsals Fred used the record to practise his steps. The number runs for seven minutes and took weeks of planning and careful editing.

It takes place on stage in a shoe shop set. Fred

sees off a satisfied customer and then finds the shoes in his shop gradually taking on personalities of their own. When he tries on a pair he finds he can't stop tapping. When others come alive he finds himself in a running battle with the disembodied shoes which threaten to overrun the shop. It's a scintillating number that ends with Fred, first with broom, then with pistols, destroying the shoes one by one.

The number was photographed with dancers wearing black tights and white shoes performing before black velvet so that only their shoes would show on film. Fred would then go through his routine carefully measuring each step, pose and movement so that when it came to joining the two sequences with process photography his movements and those of the shoes would match exactly. It remains a *tour de force* and was shot rather like a part-animated, part-live action Disney feature when cartoon figures and humans combine in one sequence.

Filming of *The Barkleys Of Broadway* proceeded painlessly except for one unfortunate incident when Judy Garland managed to slip past a security guard and arrived on set in one of the costumes she had originally been measured for. As Fred and Ginger performed on stage she began hurling insults at Ginger. In fact, so loud did they become that Ginger fled to her dressing-room. The crew became embarrassed and Chuck Walters, anxious not to make too much of the incident, asked Judy quietly if she would leave. She refused and became even louder. In the end, Walters had to take her arm and march her from the set. It was an unfortunate and unpleasant scene.

When *The Barkleys Of Broadway* was released in May 1949 Bosley Crowther wrote in *The New York Times*: 'Age cannot wither indeed – Ginger and Fred are a couple with incorruptible style. They still have that gift of mutual timing in absolute unison, so that they're always clicking together, when dancing or trifling with the plot . . . watching them spin in rapturous rhythm to the lilt of "They Can't Take That Away From Me", the old Gershwin hit, renews one's fervor for the

magic which they create. Age cannot wither the enchantment of Ginger and Fred.'

It was a nice review, of course, but one feels that nostalgia rather than objective criticism perhaps got the better of Mr Crowther that day for *The Barkleys Of Broadway*, although successful, did not go on to break any box-office records. If MGM had any ideas of teaming Fred and Ginger in another series they were quickly disillusioned. The film grossed 5\frac{1}{2}$ million, an OK figure but nothing out of the ordinary. The enchantment of the pair as a team obviously *had* worn off especially when it was remembered that *Easter Parade* had taken 1\frac{1}{2}$ million more at the box office. Fred and Ginger never danced on screen again. Their very last number on film was 'Manhattan Downbeat', the song that closed *The Barkleys Of Broadway*.

There was always a friendly rivalry between Fred and Gene Kelly during the golden period of the late 1940s and early 1950s. Who came out of things the best at MGM is difficult to say. In the end it was probably about 50/50 which is as it

should have been but it's interesting to check on who came out top in the various years. 1948, of course, belonged firmly to Fred. It could hardly have been otherwise with Gene laid up with a broken ankle. 1949, on the other hand, was Gene's year. It was then that, together with Frank Sinatra and Jules Munshin and three girls he went *On The Town* and helped create one of the classic musicals of all time. Compared with that brilliant musical extravaganza *The Barkleys Of Broadway* was something of a charming, old-fashioned also-ran.

In 1950 things came out about even. Gene danced with Judy Garland (then trying to get to grips with herself yet again) in *Summer Stock* while Fred enjoyed a change of pace in *Three Little Words*, a pleasant little biography of composers Bert Kalmar and Harry Ruby. Fred played Bert and Red Skelton played Harry.

The film was more of a singing movie than a dance musical but Fred did manage to get to do a nifty number (with Vera-Ellen) to 'Mr and Mrs Hoofer At Home' and also and with the same

Fred versus 'Shoes With Wings On' in one of the most dazzlingly inventive of all his solo routines in The Barkleys Of Broadway *(MGM, 1949).*

. . . and after the exhilaration, the let down. Fred exhausted after his battle with the shoes in The Barkleys Of Broadway *(MGM, 1949).*

Fred and Ginger and 'They Can't Take That Away From Me', a reprise of the number they first danced to in Shall We Dance? *in 1937 and the only one of their routines that they ever repeated on screen (MGM, 1949).*

partner, 'Thinking Of You!' A whole range of Kalmar/Ruby songs were included, among them the film's title song, 'I Love You So Much', 'So Long Oo-long' (sung by Fred and Red Skelton), the delightful 'Nevertheless' and 'My Sunny Tennessee'. The film was also noteworthy for giving a very young Debbie Reynolds her first break in movies.

Three Little Words was a Grade B Metro musical. That's to say it wasn't an Arthur Freed production and it wasn't directed by Vincente Minnelli. Instead, it was directed by Richard Thorpe (who had the reputation of saying 'print' after take one of every scene) and produced by Jack Cummings. A Grade C musical was usually a film

produced by Joe Pasternak and directed by either Thorpe or Robert Z. Leonard or Norman Taurog. Grade C musicals were generally all singing musicals featuring Mario Lanza or Kathryn Grayson or Jane Powell. They were rarely produced by Freed who preferred to concentrate on musicals that were big and bright and combined inventive choreography with song and dazzling set design.

If you starred in a Freed musical you knew you were at the top of the tree at Metro and although the movies produced by Cummings and Pasternak were all profitable and sometimes produced the occasional classic (such as *Kiss Me Kate* and *Seven Brides For Seven Brothers*) it was more often than not those four magical words 'An Arthur Freed

Fred and Ginger in The Barkleys Of Broadway *(MGM, 1949), their final film together and their only picture in colour.*

125

Above: 'Manhattan
Downbeat', Fred and
Ginger's final screen dance
in The Barkleys Of
Broadway (MGM,
1949).

Production' that signified quality at Culver City. *Three Little Words* marked the only occasion that Fred appeared in a postwar musical that was *not* produced by Arthur Freed.

Fred also appeared in another musical in 1950. It's one that is generally forgotten even by the most devoted of musical admirers partly because it is now rarely seen but mainly because, by any standards, it was a poor film. And, as he had done so frequently in the past, Fred strayed over to Paramount to make it. His co-star was Betty Hutton, the singer-comedienne who had been a big box-office attraction for Paramount in the war years but who was coming to the end of her reign.

The film was called *Let's Dance*. Its story was about a pair of wartime entertainers (Fred and Betty) who split up when Betty's flier husband is killed in action. They meet up again after five years, make a come-back and fight the attempts of Betty's mother-in-law to steal away Betty's son.

The pairing of Fred and Betty Hutton has been called one of the great screen mismatches of all time and although Fred, in his usual courteous manner, had some kind things to say about working with his effervescent co-star, there's no doubt that *Let's Dance* was an unfortunate mistake, both

for him and for Betty.

The pair did manage to get something out of a comedy cowboy routine called 'Oh, Them Dudes' and Fred had an enjoyable solo on and around a piano but that was about the extent of things. For the rest, *Let's Dance* was forgettable.

Three Little Words was released in July 1950, *Let's Dance* in August. In March of that year, while both films were in the cutting rooms, Fred was presented with a special, honorary Academy Award. The inscription read 'For the artistry that has brought a unique delight to picture audiences and has raised the standard of all musical pictures'.

And never was an award more merited. The Oscar Academy has never given out Oscars for singing or dancing or even, except on isolated occasions, choreography. It certainly should have done in those golden years but at least, for Fred, an honorary award was better than none. And if the citation seemed to indicate that the Academy thought that at 50 his best days might be over (an understandable view) Fred himself had other ideas. For the next seven years Fred Astaire, aged 50 to 57, would dance with some of the best dancers in Hollywood and enjoy the greatest years of his career.

Opposite: 'Where Did
You Get That Girl?'
Fred with Vera-Ellen in
Three Little Words
(MGM, 1950).

126

Opposite: *Fred and Betty Hutton perform Frank Loesser's 'Oh, Them Dudes' in Paramount's* Let's Dance *(1950)*.

Right: *Fred as lyricist Bert Kalmar, Vera-Ellen and Red Skelton as composer Harry Ruby in MGM's musical biography* Three Little Words *(MGM, 1950)*.

Below: *Fred and Vera-Ellen perform 'Mr and Mrs Hoofer At Home' in the 1950 musical* Three Little Words *(MGM)*.

Opposite: *Fred with one of his most unlikely screen partners, Betty Hutton, in Paramount's* Let's Dance *(1950).*

Left: *Fred about to get to work on the 'Piano Dance' in* Let's Dance, *choreographed by Hermes Pan at Paramount in 1950.*

STEPPING OUT WITH MY BABIES

Royal Wedding (MGM, 1951). Fred's famous ceiling and walls dance, a trick sequence filmed in just one afternoon at MGM's Culver City Studios.

As far as MGM was concerned there was no doubt that, musically speaking, 1951 was Gene Kelly's year. He starred in and helped choreograph the Vincente Minnelli musical *An American In Paris* which became the first musical since *The Broadway Melody* (released in 1929) to win an Academy Award as best film of the year.

There was certainly no way Fred could match that but he did manage to achieve something that no dancer had ever accomplished before. He appeared to dance on the walls and on the ceiling!

The ceiling dance was performed to the number 'You're All The World To Me' in the film *Royal Wedding* (retitled *Wedding Bells* in the United Kingdom). The movie was about a brother and sister dancing team who travel to England for the wedding of Princess Elizabeth and Prince Philip and themselves find love and happiness on the other side of the Atlantic. Corny stuff but once again the story was of little consequence. Alan Jay Lerner came up with the 'original' idea, basing it on Fred and Adele Astaire's personal life together and especially Adele's marriage to Lord Cavendish.

The filming of the ceiling dance remained something of a mystery for years although in fact the actual shooting was not as complicated as it might have seemed. Director Stanley Donen and art director Jack Martin Smith were the ones who worked out the mechanics. They modelled the sequence on a revolving drum principle that was used way back in the silent days in a Lupino Lane comedy called *Movieland*.

The entire room and its contents – furniture, lamps, carpets, etc – was built inside a huge cube. Everything in the room was securely fastened down. As Fred danced the cube rotated through 360 degrees (the camera turning with it) so that during the number Fred seemed to be dancing on the walls and the ceiling. Even today it remains a remarkably well photographed and skilful number. So methodically was it planned and laid out that director Stanley Donen shot the whole sequence in half a day.

Perhaps the man who had the most uncomfortable time during the filming was the camera operator. He was strapped on to an ironing board, the camera tied on to him and away they went together in a complete circle photographing Fred from every angle.

Strangely, the filming of 'You're All The World To Me' created less of a problem for Fred and MGM than the choice of his leading lady.

The first choice was June Allyson with whom Fred had never worked and who was then one of the sweethearts of movie audiences all over the world. She was also the sweetheart of her then husband Dick Powell and after a week of rehearsing 'Ev'ry Night At Seven' with Fred regretfully she had to say 'Sorry, but I'm pregnant' and bow out. Those seven days in rehearsal marked the only time she ever danced with Fred. The opportunity never came her way again.

Chuck Walters, who was the first choice as director, began looking around the star-studded MGM lot for a replacement. But when he discovered that Arthur Freed had once again settled on Judy Garland (her last chance!) he threw in the towel. He had already aged considerably (and given himself an ulcer) during the filming of Judy's recently finished movie *Summer Stock* and he had no wish to go through the experience again. Her nervous illnesses and weight problems were not only too much for her, they were also too much for just about everyone around her.

Freed accepted Walters' reasons and hired instead Stanley Donen who had worked with Gene Kelly on *On The Town*. It was Donen's first solo musical engagement.

The 'musical chairs' aspect of the filming of *Royal Wedding* gives some idea of the frustrations that could occur when filming a musical at a major Hollywood studio in the 1950s. It also demonstrates how admirably placed studios were to meet just about every crisis. Strength in depth in every aspect of moviemaking – stars, directors, composers, art directors – was the key to the smooth running of the well oiled dream factories, MGM most of all.

Not that the problems were over on *Royal Wedding* when Judy Garland and Stanley Donen replaced June Allyson and Charles Walters. There was still another change to come. And it involved Judy. Fred, who by now was getting a bit restless over all the delay, was delighted to have Judy back and be working with her again. But there were doubts in his mind as to whether she would last the

Above: *Fred and co-star Jane Powell as a brother and sister dance team who find romance when they travel to Britain in* Royal Wedding *(MGM, 1951).*

course, just as there were doubts in the minds of everyone on the crew.

Things went smoothly for the first week. During the second week arranger Saul Chaplin worked with her on her vocals and at the end of the third week Arthur Freed threw a birthday party for her on the rehearsal stage.

The trouble began during week four. Judy told Stanley Donen that she was beginning to feel the strain and that she doubted whether she could rehearse in the morning *and* the afternoon and be in a proper condition to start the movie. It was a problem for Donen. There weren't many days of rehearsals left and shooting was due to start in the near future. He begged her to reconsider the situation. Her answer was 'Take it or leave it'.

Arthur Freed came into the picture and agreed to let her rehearse just in the afternoons. It was a gesture from a man who had shown Judy loyalty all through her musical career at MGM. But it was a final gesture. On Saturday 17 June 1950 Judy rang and said she would not be coming in to rehearse.

Right: *'I Left My Hat In Haiti' – Fred, Jane Powell and full MGM chorus in* Royal Wedding *(MGM, 1951).*

134

Poor Fred was left stranded. Shooting was now imminent. Freed again intervened. This time he terminated Judy's contract. The date was 19 June 1950. Judy never worked for Metro-Goldwyn-Mayer again.

All of which meant that Fred was again left high and dry. Earlier in the proceedings someone had suggested that Moira Shearer, the British star of *The Red Shoes* might have been an appropriate choice as a partner. Fred had admitted that she was wonderful but couldn't imagine himself dancing with her. Now, he was beginning to wonder whether he had been right in his decision.

The Monday after Judy's dismissal MGM came up with a third leading lady – Jane Powell. And this time she stayed. She was more a singer than a dancer but she threw herself into things with enthusiasm which impressed Fred as did the fact that she was very tiny, eight inches shorter than he. Her top song in the movie was 'Too Late Now' which earned an Academy Award nomination and was composed, like the others in the picture, by Burton Lane and Alan Jay Lerner.

Fred's top numbers included the memorable 'Sunday Jumps' in which he performs miracles with a hatstand and his nonsense duet with Powell, 'How Could You Believe Me When I Said I Loved You When You Know I've Been A Liar All My Life!' Legend has it that this last number was created during a short car journey. In a moment of inspiration Lerner mentioned the title in one breath and Burton Lane simply hummed the tune.

Musically, *Royal Wedding* ranks with Fred's better films at MGM and looks and sounds more impressive now than it did at the time of its initial release. But in 1951 it came in the wake of *An American In Paris* and *Show Boat* and in comparison with those two blockbusters its critical reception was decidedly on the cool side.

Something Fred was constantly wondering about in 1951 was whether he was ever going to get another chance to work with Vincente Minnelli, the director of *An American In Paris* and the undisputed king of musical directors, both at

Below: *A great dancer but not so hot as a street cleaner in turn-of-the century New York. Fred in a scene from MGM's 1952 musical* The Belle Of New York.

Opposite: *'Seeing's Believing' – Fred and Vera-Ellen romantically teamed for the second time in* The Belle Of New York *(MGM, 1952).*

Left: *'Thank You Mr Currier, Thank You Mr Ives' – Fred and Vera-Ellen in* The Belle Of New York *(MGM, 1952).*

MGM and other studios. Fred had worked with him twice before of course, and on neither occasion had the pairing been a great success. *Ziegfeld Follies* had been no more than a revue and *Yolanda And The Thief* an experiment that had failed. So far, at least, Gene Kelly with *The Pirate* and *An American In Paris* had had the better of things as far as Minnelli was concerned.

It was not Minnelli who was assigned to direct Fred's next musical *The Belle Of New York* (1952). Instead it was Fred's old friend Chuck Walters who by then had worked with Fred more often than any other director at MGM. The project, of course, was the one that Fred had been cool about back in the mid-1940s and he was no more enthusiastic about it in 1952. Nor was Walters. When he later tried to pinpoint its lack of success he said that he felt there was no chemistry between Fred and his leading lady, Vera-Ellen. There certainly should have been, for Vera-Ellen was one of the most accomplished dancers of the postwar years as she had demonstrated several times, most notably in the 'Miss Turnstiles Ballet' with Kelly in *On The Town*. But for some reason, on *The Belle Of New York*, things didn't seem to gel.

Perhaps it was because everyone concerned with the production knew that the material (even though it boasted eight new songs) was rather old hat and that a turn-of-the-century tale about a New York playboy who has left five brides waiting at the altar and falls for a pretty young Salvation Army worker wasn't exactly going to set the world on fire. When a feeling like that permeates the making of a movie it's unlikely that the movie will turn out to be a great success.

Whether there were any vibes or rumours flying around on set when the film began shooting is not clear but the fact that the Kelly/Donen masterpiece *Singin' In The Rain* went into production on exactly the same day may have accounted for some of the trepidation. Not that anyone could have known in advance that *Singin' In The Rain* was going to be something special. Or could they? A huge sound stage is a small place sometimes.

The upshot was that Fred found himself appearing once again in a film that fell way below the standards of his rival even though he himself was, as usual, superb.

His highspot in the film (literally) was the 'Seeing's Believing' number in which he danced over the Washington Square Arch and the rooftops of New York and into the clouds with Vera-Ellen. He was also in top form in his speciality number 'Oops' in which he dances through a horse-drawn trolley car and 'Thank You Mr Currier, Thank You Mr Ives' in which he dances through the four seasons with Ellen against backgrounds in the style of the Currier and Ives paintings. Then there was the memorable 'I Wanna Be A Dancin' Man' and Vera-Ellen's solo (dubbed by Anita Ellis) 'Baby Doll' which made it into the hit parade.

In fact, in retrospect *The Belle Of New York*, like *Royal Wedding*, looks better now than it did at the time of its first release. Even Fred, who had such reservations about it before and during shooting later came to regard it as one of his favourite pictures. He felt the song and dance numbers by Warren and Mercer were among the best he ever

The press ad for Fred's greatest musical at MGM, The Band Wagon.

worked with and was sorry that the idea of combining fantasy sequences with a story of old New York didn't come off. And it certainly didn't come off as far as the paying public were concerned. It cost over $2½ million to produce and grossed under $2 million. It was one of the first signs that the MGM musical, even the MGM Arthur Freed musical, was not an imperishable commodity and that eventually and perhaps sooner than many people thought, the golden days would come to an end.

During his four-year stint at Metro, Fred's life continued as usual. He still liked his solitude, he preferred the company of Phyllis to anyone else's, and when he did go out to dine it was invariably only with close friends such as David Niven and Cole Porter. He hated parties and rarely attended them. Hermes Pan used to say that if you could get Fred to a party it was considered the social event of the year.

Fred preferred his house and his ranch where he was now growing oranges and grapefruit as well as raising horses. He had high hopes of Triplicate's younger daughter Stripteaser and although those hopes were never fully realised he nonetheless had great times with the horse and in between takes on set would bring out snapshots and show them to his co-stars, as though they were photographs of his children.

He also relaxed a great deal on his ranch. He played jazz records there, worked out feverishly on his set of drums and considered future projects at his leisure. He certainly didn't accept them all. When Betty Comden and Adolph Green came out to the ranch with a project called *Strategy Of Love*, he shook his head. The script was based on a fourteenth-century guide to romance. Comden and Green, enthusiastic about the idea, had updated it into the 1950s and centred it on a television writer who attempts to woo a young girl. The reason Fred said no wasn't so much because he didn't like the idea, it was more because he was getting increasingly worried about co-starring with young women. The older he got the younger they seemed to get. It was the only thing that worried him in those days of the early 1950s and it was a problem that faced many of the established stars, not all of them musical, people like Gary Cooper and Spencer Tracy, even his old friend Bing.

One project that Comden and Green brought to the ranch did make Fred sit up and take notice, however. And on this occasion he was prepared to overlook the fact that his co-star Cyd Charisse was only in her early 30s and looked like another of those women who might be a little on the tall side. The project was that good. What is more, it was to be directed by Vincente Minnelli. Its title was *The Band Wagon* (1953) and although it had little in common with the stage hit Fred had enjoyed with Adele back in the 1920s it had more potential than any other film Fred had been associated with since his return to MGM.

Its story was of a washed-up film star who sells

up in Hollywood and heads for Broadway to star, he hopes, in a new show especially written by a couple of song-writing friends. A Broadway producer with four hits currently running in New York takes on the project but turns the show into a modern version of *Faust* and also into a commercial disaster. Fred, with the help of his leading lady, ballerina Cyd Charisse and the rest of the gang, pulls it all together, re-stages the show as it was originally meant to have been staged and ends up with a smash hit.

Many people assumed that the figure played in *The Band Wagon* was meant to be based on Fred himself, which was nonsense. The only similarity between Fred and his fictional creation Tony Hunter was that they were both getting on a bit in years. Fred was certainly not washed up in movies before *The Band Wagon*. Anything but, in fact.

Nonetheless, it remains one of those myths that have grown up around the film. The two scriptwriters, played by Oscar Levant and Nanette Fabray, were certainly based closely on Comden and Green and there was talk of the fact that the producer (played in the film by Jack Buchanan after Clifton Webb had turned down the role) had a certain affinity with José Ferrer who at that time was having a remarkable run of success on Broadway.

The film's main asset however was that it had a superb score. Arthur Freed had already had a tremendous success with *An American In Paris* and *Singin' In The Rain*, the first of which had been entirely drawn from music by Gershwin, the second from the songbook of Freed and Nacio Herb Brown. Now it was the turn of Howard Dietz and Arthur Schwartz's songs to form the basis of a musical.

The exquisite 'Dancing In The Dark', performed by Fred and Cyd Charisse in a New York Central Park setting, in The Band Wagon *(MGM, 1953).*

Opposite: *Fred with Cyd Charisse in 'Girl Hunt' from* The Band Wagon *(MGM, 1953).*

Right: *Fred's 'A Shine On Your Shoes' number, performed in a glittering New York amusement arcade in the early reels of* The Band Wagon *(MGM, 1953).*

Below: *'Triplets' – Fred, Nanette Fabray and Jack Buchanan in* The Band Wagon *(MGM, 1953).*

It was an unusual procedure. On Broadway and in Hollywood when it came to producing original screen musicals the practice was to fit the songs around an existing story and plotline. With his three greatest ever musicals at MGM Freed turned the process on its head. He had the songs. He just thought up a story to go with them.

Thus in *An American In Paris* Gene Kelly found himself as a painter-turned-hoofer pursuing Leslie Caron and thus too in *Singin' In The Rain* he appeared as a matinée idol of the silent screen. Fred's appearance in *The Band Wagon* as a former Hollywood star trying to make a come-back on Broadway came about via the same topsy-turvy route.

Fred revelled in *The Band Wagon*. The plot allowed for several marvellous routines plus, of course, the chance to dance with Cyd Charisse. Their loveliest number is 'Dancing In The Dark' in which they are both exquisitely dressed in white, alight from a horse-drawn coach and glide through a Central Park setting. It is a number of supreme

'Girl Hunt: A Murder Mystery in Jazz'. Fred and Cyd Charisse turn up the heat in Vincente Minnelli's The Band Wagon (MGM, 1953).

elegance. Perfection is rarely attained on screen in any form but Fred and Cyd Charisse, helped by Minnelli's gentle guiding hand and his flair for colour, came close to it with 'Dancing In The Dark' in *The Band Wagon*.

Elsewhere in the film Fred kicks open a fun machine in an amusement arcade in the 'A Shine On Your Shoes' number, strolls down a station platform humming 'By Myself', duets with Buchanan in top hat, white tie and tails to 'I Guess I'll Have To Change My Plan' and even goes down on his knees and dresses up, along with Nanette Fabray and Jack Buchanan, as tiny babies in the comedy song 'Triplets'.

This last named number was painful to perform for it meant all three artistes moving forward on their knees and singing in time to the music. Oscar Levant was originally supposed to have participated but cried off at the last minute due to illness. Fabray knelt in for him.

In fact, Mr Levant's constant worries about his health often brought about friction on the set. Vincente Minnelli eventually lost patience and said: 'Snap out of it Oscar. There's nothing the matter with you, it's all in your mind!' to which Levant, horrified, replied: 'In my mind, what a terrible place to be!'

The one new number compiled by Schwartz and Dietz for *The Band Wagon* was the climactic 'That's Entertainment'. Freed had asked if they could come up with a 'There's No Business Like Show Business'-type number for the finale. Just 30

minutes after the request was made the composers produced 'That's Entertainment'.

The most exhilarating (and the sexiest) moment in *The Band Wagon* comes during the ballet 'Girl Hunt: A Murder Mystery In Jazz'. The number is a spoof of the Mickey Spillane detective novels that were so popular at the time. It opens with machine-gun bullets ripping into the jacket of a trashy pulp novel. Fred, clad in white suit and hat, brown shirt and white tie, ambles on. He lights a cigarette and in an off-screen narration (written uncredited by Alan Jay Lerner) begins his story. 'My name's Rod Riley. I'm a detective. I'd just finished a case . . .'

Before long he's into another one. It's one that involves a man who disappears in a puff of

nitroglycerine leaving behind him only a rag, a bone and a hank of hair. The sound of a lonesome horn offers Fred a clue. Then two women arrive on the scene, one a frightened blonde, the other a slinky dance-hall moll who performs in 'Dem Bones Cafe', complete with skeleton across the entrance. Both women are played by Cyd Charisse and when Fred comments on the soundtrack 'She came at me in sections: more curves than a scenic railway', one cannot but agree with him. As Cyd's moll snakes towards Fred, the scene becomes one of the most sensual ever seen in an American musical. For 3 minutes (the entire ballet runs for 13 minutes) the screen is white hot. Fred, whipping along to the jazz beat with Cyd, made *Top Hat* suddenly seem light years away. Until that

Fred and Cyd Charisse in the climax to 'Girl Hunt' from The Band Wagon *(MGM, 1953).*

Right: *Fred and his family at the Hollywood premiere of* The Band Wagon. *From left to right: Fred's mother Ann, his 11-year-old daughter Ava, Fred and his wife Phyllis.*

Below: *Orphan girl Leslie Caron falls for her wealthy benefactor (Fred) in the 1955 musical* Daddy Long Legs *(Twentieth Century-Fox).*

moment the link had always been there. But at that precise moment the romance and charm of RKO in the 1930s went out of the window. Rhythm and sex took its place.

The 'Girl Hunt' ballet was shot after the rest of the film had been completed. And it was shot in a hurry, as Cyd Charisse remembers: 'Arthur Freed said, "All right, now we have one more production number to do. The production office is very upset about the cost so it must be shot quickly". They said to me "Cyd, you have to get the scene in which you slide in on the floor and grab Fred's legs in one take. We haven't time to keep waxing the floor". So I did it on the first take. Arthur Freed had a way of applying pressure so that everyone worked flat out. At the end of six months of filming one has a tendency to let down but Arthur psyched everyone up to keep them on their toes. We did it all amazingly quickly – the effects with the camera, Fred spinning – but they had every set there already built so we just jumped from one set to another. They were lighting up the next one while we were shooting our scene. You would have thought it was a silent movie.'

Director Vincente Minnelli had told Freed that he would complete the 'Girl Hunt' ballet in three days. He went over that deadline but not by much. The final cost of *The Band Wagon* was a little over $2 million of which $300,000 went on the ballet sequence. But it was money well spent. *The Band Wagon* emerged as Fred's finest musical since *Top Hat.*

Arthur Winston in *The New York Post* of 19 July 1953 wrote: 'No mistake about it, a review of *The Band Wagon* at the Music Hall boils down to a collection of superlatives. It is the best musical of the month, the year, the decade, or, for all I know, of all time. For my money it's better than *An American In Paris* which was good enough.'

Bosley Crowther in *The New York Times* added: 'There was some instinctive hesitation in the mind of this reviewer the other day when he came out and said *The Band Wagon* might be one of the best musical films ever made. Lofty comments of that nature sometimes have a way of popping up a few weeks or months later and causing the maker's face to turn bright red. But another inspection of the picture, which is now on the Music Hall's screen, and a hasty review of the record emboldens us to let the comment stand. As a matter of fact, we'll make

Fred and the 24-year-old Leslie Caron in the 1955 CinemaScope musical Daddy Long Legs *(Twentieth Century-Fox).*

146

it stronger: it *is* one of the best musicals ever made.'

Over 30 years later that comment still holds good. *The Band Wagon* remains one of the greatest of all time, good enough to fit in with anybody's top ten, top five, conceivably top three. Together with *An American In Paris* and *Singin' In The Rain* it makes up a trio of films (made in successive years) the like of which has never been seen since. Nor is it likely that such a trio will ever be seen again. For Fred it was a moment of triumph, an artistic summit that he must have wondered if he was ever going to reach after he had left RKO. But reach it he did. The come-back out of retirement had paid rich dividends indeed.

When *The Band Wagon* opened he took his mother, Phyllis and Ava to the premiere. All of them enjoyed the film and none of them had any worries about the future. Fred had completed his contract with MGM but there seemed to be every possibility of more films on the horizon. Neither Fred nor his mother nor Phyllis had any premonition of what was to come and it was both ironic and terribly sad that at the moment of his greatest triumph, Fred should for the first time in his life suffer a personal heartache that was almost unbearable.

The first indications that something was amiss occurred at the Santa Anita race-track when in the middle of the afternoon Phyllis asked to be taken home because of a splitting headache. The headache lasted for a bit but although Fred was concerned he thought it to be no more than a migraine, especially as it appeared to clear up as quickly as it had come.

Just before the following Easter however Phyllis fell ill again, once more while at a race-track. This time she felt bad enough to call off going to a dinner party being given by Cole Porter. That night her condition got worse and she decided on seeing a doctor. He ordered x-rays to be taken immediately. The x-rays disclosed a spot on her lung that was found to be malignant.

On Good Friday 1954, Phyllis was admitted to hospital and underwent an operation. This was followed five hours later by a second operation, resulting in a large section of her lung being removed.

When Phyllis came out of hospital she and Fred retired quietly to the ranch. To Fred's relief she seemed to improve as the days and the weeks went by. The radiation treatments she had been undergoing seemed successful, Fred Jr, who had requested special leave from his air force base in Texas, returned to his unit and even the nurse who had been employed by Fred to look after her daily needs was sent home. But any hopes that Fred might have entertained that Phyllis was going to get well were quickly dashed in the autumn. In September she suffered a serious relapse and underwent another operation. She stayed in a coma for weeks and never came round. On 13 September she died, aged just 46.

Until that moment Fred had lived a life that was blessedly free from personal tragedy. Now he was beside himself. He and Phyllis had been close for over 20 years. They had always been together, there was never the hint of a breakdown in their marriage, they had always been blissfully happy in each other's company. Now Phyllis was gone and Fred was alone. The future was bleak, meaningless. Work was out of the question, at least for a while. And even after weeks and months of grief he was still unable to pull himself round. When friends tentatively suggested that a film, or even work of any kind might help in some way, he quickly quashed any such ideas.

But in the end, work was the only way out. Before the death of Phyllis Fred had signed to make a musical for Twentieth Century-Fox. Its title was *Daddy Long Legs* and it was based on the 1912 novel by Jean Webster (who had also turned it into a play) about a wealthy businessman who anonymously sponsors an orphan girl's education. The story had been filmed twice before – in 1919 when Mary Pickford and Mahlon Hamilton had played the leads, and 1931 when Janet Gaynor and Warner Baxter starred in a Fox production.

The 1955 film was directed by Jean Negulesco, not a director known for his musicals but an accomplished film maker nonetheless. The plotline was altered slightly so that the film could have a partly French, partly American setting. This was to accommodate the fact that Fred's leading lady (the orphan he takes under his wing) was 22-year-old Leslie Caron.

As a film *Daddy Long Legs* was a long way from *The Band Wagon* class but it did have its moments, especially when Fred sang the Oscar-nominated Johnny Mercer song 'Something's Gotta Give' and then dances sublimely with Caron on a hotel balcony. Fred also dances with Leslie in the 'with-it' 1950s number 'The Sluefoot' in which they were backed by the Ray Anthony orchestra, and in two dream ballets – 'Daydream Sequence' and 'Dancing Through Life', both of them choreographed by Roland Petit.

The film's main drawback was that it was photographed in the letter-box shaped Cinema-Scope process which didn't exactly help the design of the musical numbers. Neither did the fact that the film was shot in the DeLuxe colour process which Fox had adopted as a replacement for Technicolor. DeLuxe colour turned every other scene into pastel shaded pinks and blues and mauves. Another problem was that the Cinema-Scope process was then still in its infancy which meant there were problems in the corners of the screen with the luckless actors sometimes appearing squashed up and extra thin. Fred wasn't exactly a heavyweight but whenever he floated across to the edge of a CinemaScope screen he was sometimes in danger of vanishing altogether!

Still, no film co-starring that slow-burn comedian Fred Clark (as Fred's business manager) and that beloved 'Call-a-spade-a-spade' New Yorker

Overleaf: *Fred as a sophisticated man of the world in the 'International Playboy' dance sequence in* Daddy Long Legs *(Twentieth Century-Fox, 1955).*

Opposite: *Fred's drumming ability does not impress his business manager (played by character actor Fred Clark). A scene from* Daddy Long Legs *(Twentieth Century-Fox, 1955).*

Thelma Ritter (as Fred's secretary) could be entirely swallowed up by an imperfect technical process and Fred himself was glad to have made the picture. He later commented: 'That helped. It's a hard thing to accept it and have to be as busy as I was. I was working with Leslie Caron and the picture was good. I loved the movie, and was glad to be able to do it. There was a lot of work to do, so the only thing was that there would be a reaction later on.'

Daddy Long Legs remained the only musical Fred ever made at Fox, a pity perhaps for he might well have fitted into some of their subsequent projects. But it was not to be. While he was making it, he managed as he said to lose himself in work. But once it was finished, his sense of loss returned.

Fox did in fact announce him for another project, one called *Dry Martini*, but it never materialised. Neither did a film he was due to make at Paramount with the same team that had been responsible for *Daddy Long Legs* — director Jean Negulesco and writers Henry and Phoebe Ephron.

Its title was *Papa's Delicate Condition* and it was to be a comedy with music about the boozy father of silent film star Corinne Griffith. Johnny Mercer who with *Daddy Long Legs* had proved his versatility by writing both the lyrics and the music, was not this time called upon to write the score. Instead, Sammy Cahn and Jimmy Van Heusen were asked to come up with the songs.

Sammy, whose long cherished ambition had been to write a score for a Fred Astaire movie, has vivid memories of the assignment: 'When I was a young budding songwriter on the east coast, one of the great goals of my life was to write for Fred Astaire. Fred was *the* goal and I used to say to myself that if I ever got to California and if I was

Funny Face.
Paramount's musical fairy tale of a magazine photographer who takes a young Greenwich Village bookseller to Paris and turns her into a fashion model. Fred's co-star — Audrey Hepburn (Paramount, 1957).

Funny Face
*(Paramount, 1957).
Fred with Audrey
Hepburn in Paris.*

ever successful enough to get to a Hollywood studio, Fred Astaire would be my aim.

'I thought he would be long gone before that dream was ever achieved but then one day the phone rang and there they were asking me to write a score for Fred Astaire. I just went absolutely berserk. One of the first ideas I came up with was "Call Me Irresponsible" which dealt with the delicate condition of the father, you know, he was irresponsible, completely irresponsible. I said to Van Heusen, we've got to play this song right away for Fred Astaire.

'Well he couldn't understand how I wanted to stand in front of Fred Astaire more than anything in life. He said "What's the hurry, we've only just started this assignment?" I said, "What do you mean, what's the hurry? If this song isn't correct for this film then we're not correct," and I just badgered him and badgered him until he said OK.

'Came the magic moment. I stood in front of

Fred Astaire. It was one of the great, great moments of my life. When people say to me, "Who is the most incredible song salesman you've ever met", I'm supposed to say Sinatra. But it's Fred Astaire. You know why? Because with him the word stands in front of the note. The trouble with most singers is that they sing more than they enunciate. You hear singing, you don't hear lyrics. But Fred Astaire is one of the single best lyric enunciators. His record for introducing songs is incomparable. There's no-one comes near him for introducing songs by the most famous writers.

'Anyway, so there I was, standing in front of Fred Astaire about to sing a song. I set up the scene, I told him how the song would happen and I started to sing. And he said, "Stop!" I thought Van Heusen would fall off the piano bench. Fred said "That is one of the best songs I've ever heard". I said, "Excuse me, Mr Astaire, that is one of the best *half* songs you have ever heard. If you'll allow

Funny Face
(Paramount, 1957), the
most sophisticated of all
Fred's movie musicals.
His co-star – Audrey
Hepburn. The music – by
George Gershwin and
Roger Edens.

Kay Thompson joins a
bearded guitar-playing
Fred in 'Clap Yo'
Hands', a send-up of the
beatnik generation in
Funny Face
(Paramount, 1957).

MGM's press advertisement for Silk Stockings *(1957), Cole Porter's musical reworking of the 1939 Garbo movie,* Ninotchka.

M-G-M Presents AN ARTHUR FREED PRODUCTION

Starring FRED ASTAIRE · CYD CHARISSE

Silk Stockings

Also Co Starring

JANIS PAIGE · PETER LORRE with JULES MUNSHIN · GEORGE TOBIAS · JOSEPH BULOFF

Screen Play by LEONARD GERSHE and LEONARD SPIGELGASS

COLE PORTER Based on the Original Musical Play by GEORGE S. KAUFMAN, LEUEEN McGRATH and ABE BURROWS

in CinemaScope and METROCOLOR Directed by ROUBEN MAMOULIAN

me to finish please". So I finished the song and he repeated that he thought it was incredibly good. We were just so happy because we knew we had a good song.

'As we got up to go he said to me, "Do you know how you happened to get this assignment?" I said, "No". He said with a laugh "Because Johnny Mercer wasn't available". I said, "I consider that a high compliment, Mr Astaire". He said, "No, I will now give you the compliment. The compliment is that the next time Mercer leaves town I won't be nervous."'

Paramount obviously were nervous, however, for the movie, although it looked as though it was all set for production, didn't get off the ground. Not in the 1950s anyway and not with Fred Astaire. It was eventually filmed in 1963 with Jackie Gleason (a fine actor but not exactly Fred Astaire) in the role of the father. The song that Sammy Cahn had sung to Fred that day at Paramount studios lay dormant for something like seven years. But both Fred and Sammy were proved right about its quality. In 1963 it was awarded an Oscar as the best song of the year.

The mid-1950s proved to be the most difficult period in Fred's life. He felt as though he was in a kind of limbo. He knew that he was now alone but couldn't really come to terms with the fact. His loneliness drew him closer to his mother and his daughter Ava. In July 1955 the three of them paid a visit to Europe for a holiday but Fred was content to stay quietly within the walls of Lismore Castle in Ireland rather than to go sightseeing. He did start escorting Ava, who was then 13, to the odd film premiere or two which was as much a treat for a young girl on the threshold of her teens as it was company for a Hollywood star.

Paramount (so long his hoodoo studio) came to the rescue as far as work was concerned. They signed him to make a couple of films for them in three years. One in which he was set to co-star once more with Bing Crosby fell through because Bing and Paramount parted company shortly after the project was announced. The other, however, went ahead. The film's title was *Funny Face* (1957) and Fred's co-star was 27-year-old Audrey Hepburn.

It was not a film version of the Broadway stage show of the 1920s, the one in which Fred had co-starred with Adele. But it did contain much of the original show's Gershwin music plus some original numbers by Roger Edens and Leonard Gershe. It was based on a show called *Wedding Day* which had never been performed and which its author Leonard Gershe thought might make a good movie.

He was right. It made a superb movie even though no-one seemed anxious to get it off the ground to begin with. Originally it had been an MGM project with Roger Edens set to produce, Stanley Donen to direct and many of the Freed unit employed on the technical side. MGM's idea was to get Fred on loan from Paramount and star him

with Audrey who had just finished making the huge spectacular *War and Peace* and was more than eager to appear in something light and fluffy. Rumour has it that she was supposed to have said, 'This is the part I've been waiting 27 years for, to dance with Fred Astaire'. Which was great news for her but more than a little disconcerting for Fred who was then 30 years her senior.

The upshot of all the haggling between MGM and Paramount was that Paramount said, 'No, Metro couldn't have Fred on loan'. Whereupon MGM sold the whole package to Paramount, including Hepburn and, just for the one film, Edens, Donen and the rest. The result was, of course, a musical that looked like an MGM film through and through but which rather uncannily bore the Paramount trade-mark.

Fred's role was that of a magazine fashion photographer who is taken with the young girl he finds working in a Greenwich Village bookshop, then whisks her across to Paris to transform her into a glamorous model. It was a Cinderella-type story that also managed to take a few satirical swipes at two of the fads of the 1950s – the ridiculous excesses and superficiality of high fashion magazines (especially their preoccupations with the colour pink, an 'in' colour during the period) and the Beat Generation who rejected the American Dream and dropped out of society.

Where it scored most though was in its superb song and dance numbers, all of them brilliantly photographed in rich and sometimes hazy mellow colours by cameraman Ray June. In fact, it's doubtful whether colour has ever been more effectively used in a movie musical. Visually, *Funny Face* is ravishing. And never more so than when Fred sings 'I Love Your Funny Face' to Audrey in a sequence that is photographed entirely in red in a photographic darkroom.

Running it close is the 'Basal Metabolism' number danced by Audrey in the cellars of a smoky Paris bistro, the 'Think Pink' sequence which dazzles the eye with its images of delicious pink-clad girls and the memorable 'He Loves And She Loves' to which Fred serenades Audrey on the banks of the Seine in a scene that is so deftly photographed through filters and gauze that the screen simply glows with a soft delicacy.

Said director Stanley Donen: 'Since it was a movie about fashion photography, the use of colour became very important, almost of primary importance.' So too did the director's inventiveness when he photographed the 'Bonjour Paris' number and split the screen three ways as he followed his three main characters, all of them taking separate tourist routes around Paris. It was no accident that Donen had helped Gene Kelly direct the marvellous opening 'New York, New York' number in *On The Town*!

Funny Face, which also included the numbers 'Let's Kiss And Make Up', 'How Long Has This Been Going On?' and 'Clap Yo' Hands' (sung by Fred and Kay Thompson as Fred's editress), stands

'Fated To Be Mated' Fred and Cyd Charisse in Silk Stockings. *Said Fred of his partner, 'When you've danced with her you stay danced with!' (MGM, 1957).*

Fred and Janis Paige and
the exhuberant
'Stereophonic Sound'
number in Silk Stockings
(MGM, 1957).

with *The Band Wagon* as one of the greatest musicals Fred made away from RKO. That it should have been directed by Stanley Donen, who had first worked with Fred on *Royal Wedding*, was perhaps poetic justice. *Royal Wedding* had been fine musically but had an indifferent plot. *Funny Face* had it all.

Fred was flattering about Audrey's musical talents. Half a century later she returned the compliment when she paid tribute to him at a gala occasion to celebrate Fred's Lifetime Achievement Award for his unique contribution to film. She recalled her first meeting with Fred at rehearsals for *Funny Face*. 'I remember he was wearing a yellow shirt, grey flannels, a red scarf knotted around his waist instead of a belt, and the famous feet were clad in soft moccasins and pink socks. He was also wearing that irresistible smile.

'One look at this most debonair, elegant and distinguished of legends and I could feel myself turn

to solid lead, while my heart sank into my two left feet. Then suddenly I felt a hand around my waist and, with his inimitable grace and lightness, Fred literally swept me off my feet. I experienced the thrill that all women at some point in their lives have dreamed of – to dance just once with Fred Astaire.'

The critics were kind to *Funny Face*. One however did pass a comment that sank home with Fred. Three years later he remembered it: 'I was determined not to become a dancing freak at 60. I knew the time had come to quit when one critic said of *Funny Face* that it had "something old" and "something new". I was the "something old!"'

This may well have been part of the reason he was reluctant to take on another assignment for producer Arthur Freed when Freed approached him to appear in his film version of Cole Porter's Broadway hit *Silk Stockings*. Porter's musical was based on the 1939 Garbo movie hit *Ninotchka*, about a stiff, strait-laced Russian commissar who falls in love with an American businessman and is transformed under his influence. The musical kept close to the original plot but substituted an American film director for the businessman.

Even though dance predominated in *Silk Stockings*, Fred dug his heels in firmly. He was, he told Freed, too old for the role. The prospect of working again with Cyd Charisse (who had the Garbo role) tempted him, the thought of working with director Rouben Mamoulian, a man with whom he'd never worked previously, did not. There were even those at MGM who thought that Freed was taking a bit of a chance with Mamoulian. The director had not worked since 1948 when his *Summer Holiday*, a musical version of *Ah Wilderness*, had flopped badly despite the fact that Mickey Rooney had the star part.

Still, Freed thought Mamoulian was right for *Silk Stockings*. All he had to do was to persuade Fred that he was also right for the picture. When he mentioned his problem to Mamoulian the director immediately said, 'Right, we'll sort things out. Arrange a lunch for just Fred and me.' The lunch was duly arranged and Mamoulian got to work on Fred. He told him that the only reason he had accepted the assignment was because of him and Cyd Charisse. When Fred, flattered but not convinced, started to raise the question of age, Mamoulian dismissed the age problem as non-existent. 'What kind of nonsense is that? I see all the young actors today on the screen and none of them can match you in charm or romantic appeal, so for heaven's sake, get off that peg – you're not too old!' It was quite a convincing job by Mamoulian. When he saw that Fred was beginning to waver he closed in again: 'With you, a dancer playing the film producer, and Cyd, a dancer playing the Russian girl, I think we can introduce a new element – pantomime – in place of extended dialogue. We'll have high comedy with the three Russian commissars and a love story that is believable and touching.' Fred was completely won over and signed for the role.

Silk Stockings (1957) didn't turn out quite as Mamoulian had described it. It was a long way from the class of *Funny Face* for instance. But like all Fred's films it had more than its fair share of great moments. The exquisite dance routine with Cyd Charisse to 'All Of You' belongs with his great set pieces and is Cyd's favourite of all her screen numbers. 'Fated To Be Mated' in which Cyd gradually melts to Fred's charm is another highspot, as is the witty spoof number on the new fangled screen processes 'Stereophonic Sound' which Fred performs with Janis Paige who was third-billed as a brassy Esther Williams-type swimming star.

Silk Stockings was previewed just nine days after the last shot was made, which was fast going by anybody's standards, even Arthur Freed's. Inevitably perhaps those last shots involved Fred. He had just one number left to perform entitled 'The Ritz Roll And Rock'. It had been specially composed, at Fred's request, by Cole Porter. Fred wanted a solo number in the film and Porter, although not exactly conversant with the new rock'n'roll trend, duly obliged, as he always did where Fred was concerned. In the number Fred wears top hat, white tie and tails and also a red sash. As he hits his tap routine he pays homage to the past and acknowledges the present. He seems to be saying, 'this is what I used to do, the other is what's to come, and thank you very much ladies and gentlemen, but this really is my swan song.'

As indeed it was. Fred's number on the Metro lot in January 1957 was the last time he ever appeared in a major musical on those famous stages. As he practised and rehearsed he was surely aware of the fact. It wasn't only his age, although of course that was the main problem, it was also the fact that the musical was no longer what it was. The golden age of the musical, especially the original screen musical, was already past and most of those connected with the entertainment form knew it. Rock'n'roll was only one symptom of a changing musical scene. Audiences were getting younger with each succeeding year. The middle-aged audiences were beginning to stay home more and watch television. And Fred's audience was that audience who now stayed at home and gazed not at the wonders of a big screen but the somewhat less ambitious endeavours of the television stars.

It was perhaps fitting that Fred should make his last great musical at MGM, the studio at which he had worked for ten magnificent years between 1948 and 1957. Shortly after he left Culver City the musicals came to an end at Metro. There were the occasional ones made of course, but the regular programme of films that had come out of the Arthur Freed unit for so long was suddenly halted.

Saul Chaplin, the music arranger and composer who had long been an employee at the studio, remembers the 'final cut' all too well. It happened not long after filming of *Silk Stockings* had been completed. Chaplin was working on the film *Merry Andrew* starring Danny Kaye: 'We were shooting the film and then from New York came the edict, no more musicals. We still had four songs to shoot but they said, forget it, finish the picture in two weeks. Poor Michael Kidd, whose first job as a director it was, had to find a way to finish the picture very quickly. As far as a programme of regular musicals was concerned, that was the end of it.

'They found out that musicals would make just a certain amount of money. Something like $2½ million. In other words, if you made a picture for $2 million you might get by but not beyond that. This picture was going to cost more than that so they cut it right off. They said there's no way to get our money back after this and that's the way the musicals stopped.'

In retrospect it was more than appropriate that Fred and the MGM musical came to an end at one and the same time.

Overleaf: *Fred with top hat, white tie and tails, plus a sash and a mirror in his final musical for MGM*, Silk Stockings (*1957*).

1709-1

THAT'S ENTERTAINMENT

Most people in Hollywood felt that Fred would at last retire permanently from the screen with the release of *Silk Stockings*. He had made 29 films, all of them musicals, in 24 years. And in those films he had said just about all he had to say about the art of song and dance.

Not for the first time, people guessed wrongly. Fred had no intention whatsoever of giving up work. Had Phyllis still been with him he might well have considered a relaxed retirement among the race-tracks and golf courses of California. But she wasn't and the only way Fred could forget his still poignant memories was to carry on working. He developed an interest in television and, much to people's surprise, dramatic acting.

He had, in fact, made his first appearance on television back in 1955 when he had appeared on the *Ed Sullivan Show* to help promote his film *Daddy Long Legs*. He had subsequently appeared on the Arlene Francis and Art Linkletter shows and even played the drums on the *Person To Person* programme. But most people thought these were no more than token appearances by a man who was fading out of the limelight gradually. Marie Torre in *The New York Herald Tribune* wrote: 'The recent Fred Astaire appearances on television have sprung hope in the hearts of video pursuers who have been falling over antennae trying to shake loose from the movie lots. Sad to relate, however, any TV man with Astaire in his eyes is merely having a pipe dream.'

In December 1957 Miss Torre was proved wrong. Fred appeared in a CBS television comedy with Charles Laughton called *Imp On A Cobweb Leash*. It was a fantasy by Jameson Brewer and it was a success. Fred had originally agreed to appear in a play just that once. But his excellent notices and the fact that he had appeared in his first entertainment without once singing or dancing did not go unnoticed by him. Television and he, he decided, definitely had a future together.

That future really began in 1958 when Fred was approached by the Chrysler Corporation to appear in a Fred Astaire Special. The Special was to be transmitted in colour. It would be live and David Rose would serve as musical director, fronting a 50-piece orchestra. It was one of the biggest challenges Fred had had to face since making his movie come-back in 1948.

Fred didn't take long in making up his mind. With the added proviso that he could also produce the show (through his newly formed company Ava Productions) he said yes. And with Hermes Pan also joining the package to help out with the dances it was just like old times. Almost, but not quite. There was no leading lady, no dancing partner. Fred could perform solos of course but he also needed a partner to join him in such evergreens as 'Change Partners', 'A Foggy Day' and 'Baubles, Bangles And Beads'.

The girl he eventually chose was named Barrie Chase. Fred had first noticed her in a small role in *Silk Stockings* and she had been in the business since she was three when she danced on skates with the Sonja Henie troupe. Her father was the screen-writer Borden Chase who had worked mostly on westerns in Hollywood, scripting pictures such as *Man Without A Star*, *Where The River Bends*, *Winchester 73* and *Red River*.

There was nothing very western about Barrie Chase; she was very much of the twentieth century. Fred felt she would make an ideal partner. And never did he show better judgment. Barrie Chase turned out to be the best partner he had had since Cyd Charisse and Rita Hayworth.

Long a fan of Fred's, she had two great advantages when she came to work on *An Evening With Fred Astaire*, as the show came to be called. She was short, thus making Fred appear tall. And she was a hard worker. She knew she had to be. Fred's reputation had preceded him of course. And just because he was performing on the small screen instead of the large there was no difference in his approach. It was still the same old formula: 'Work, work, work . . . practice, practice, practice.'

So hard did Fred rehearse Barrie that it was often as much as she could do to blink back the tears. Fred was not averse to shouting and cussing when things didn't go right and it was not unusual for Barrie to flee from the rehearsal room in tears. When she came back, two hours later, composed and ready to start again, Fred would ignore the incident and pretend it had never happened.

David Rose, for whom working with Fred was a new experience, found the amount of work that went into preparing the show staggering: 'I would walk into a rehearsal', he said, 'and there would be

dead silence for five minutes with Fred and Hermes Pan just staring at each other. Then Hermes would say to Fred that he had the answer to their problem. He would step off on the left foot instead of the right. They had been debating for 15 minutes which foot to step out on. Every step he took just had to be accounted for.'

The main thing concerning Fred as the October 1958 transmission date for the show approached was that it was 'live'. There was no chance to do it again if he fluffed, no safety net of retakes. It was like appearing in the theatre once more, something Fred had not done since the early 1930s.

He need not have worried. He got everything right. So too did Barrie Chase whose exciting dancing brought her instant recognition. Many critics referred to her as the best partner Fred had ever had. She did all the steps. She was graceful one minute, rhythmically exciting the next. The show achieved a rating for the network of 18.9 per cent of the total American television audience which was good enough but even that was superseded when the show was repeated in January 1959 when the rating reached 26.2 per cent.

An Evening With Fred Astaire won nine Emmy awards including one for Fred as best actor, an award which raised a few eyebrows in that most people felt a best actor award should go to a dramatic performer. But if anybody deserved an award for that historic television show (the first to be taped so that the sponsor could enjoy repeated transmissions) it was Fred. The show had taken up long arduous months to rehearse and get together. The Emmy was just reward for all the hard work.

Fred, however, didn't have to wait long for his dramatic role. Independent producer Stanley Kramer had long been wanting to film Nevil Shute's novel *On The Beach* and when at last he got the go-ahead in 1959 Fred was one of the actors he chose for a leading role. Hollywood was stunned. Fred Astaire in a dramatic role? Surely not – and in a movie about the last days of civilisation after a nuclear Third World War!

It was, of course, a long way from *Top Hat* and Fred admitted that he had doubts about taking on the assignment. His role was that of a boozy and all-too-knowing scientist whose predictions about what was to befall the few remaining survivors of the holocaust (the film was set in Australia) made chilling listening.

The casting was an astute move on Kramer's part. Casting against type always helped a film at the box office and casting Fred alongside Gregory Peck, Ava Gardner and Anthony Perkins was as shrewd a move as when former Warner singing star Dick Powell took up private-eye work in *Farewell My Lovely* back in 1944.

Fred's big scene came at the end of the movie. Determined not to await death from radiation poisoning he locks himself in his garage and chokes to death on the exhaust fumes of his car. It was a dramatic end to an impressive performance. When the film was finally in the can Fred was a

little unsure as to how he had fared. He reasoned, however, that if a director of Kramer's standing was satisfied with him as a cynical scientist then he must have carried it off reasonably well. He also felt that he must have been convincing because Kramer hadn't thrown him off the set before the film was finished!

1959, therefore, was quite a year for Fred – an Emmy award for his first television show and an 'acting debut' in one of Hollywood's most prestigious films of the year. A unique double in fact for a man who had officially retired from musical movies just a year before.

Fred was to continue (and indeed still continues) in similar vein for the next two decades. The fact

Above: *Fred with Barrie Chase, a regular dancing partner on his popular TV shows of the 1960s.*

Opposite: *Fred with Barrie Chase who was just 24 when she first danced with Fred on the TV spectacular 'An Evening With Fred Astaire'.*

Fred and Barrie Chase. Among their TV shows together: An Evening With Fred Astaire *(1958),* Astaire Time *(1960),* Hollywood Palace *(1966) and* The Fred Astaire Show *(1968).*

164

that he became 70 instead of 60 and then 80 instead of 70 seemed to make no difference. Of course, it wasn't the Fred Astaire of old. Some felt that he should have retired gracefully after *Silk Stockings* and left things at that. But Fred has never been one to dwell in the past. He has always hated to look back. He likes to live in the present. He was and always has been a workaholic so when he found that, by accident, two new parallel careers were opening up for him he seized the opportunity to embark on both with his usual enthusiasm.

Television saw the most of him in the 1960s and 1970s. He did three more specials with Barrie Chase, each and every one as exciting as the last, he appeared in single TV plays and he fronted, for two years, a weekly TV series called *Fred Astaire's Premiere Theater* in which, (like Dick Powell and Alfred Hitchcock who also had their own series), he introduced a number of widely differing plays and stories. He even appeared in a few, among them *Mister Easy, Moment Of Decision, Guest In The House, Mister Lucifer* and *Blues For A Hanging*.

Opposite top: *Fred,
shown here with Gregory
Peck and Ava Gardner,
in his first dramatic role
in* On The Beach
*(United Artists), directed
by Stanley Kramer in
1959.*

Left: *Fred occasionally
appeared in the plays he
hosted on TV in his*
Premier Theater *series.
In this scene from* Blues
For A Hanging *(1962)
he appears with Janis
Paige.*

And as if that wasn't enough, he even popped up in the popular TV series *Dr Kildare* with Richard Chamberlain and enjoyed himself in the Robert Wagner TV series *It Takes A Thief*, all about a master thief who is paroled on the condition that he works on the government's behalf among the international jet set.

The only problem with television is that, by and large, it's an instant medium, here today, gone tomorrow. Unlike film, video tape is rarely kept for posterity and repeated viewings. That matters little for the greater part of television, especially American television, is not worth keeping anyway. But it does mean that glimpses of Fred in his TV heyday in the 1960s are rare and also that his memorable musical spectaculars with Barrie Chase remain unseen by most people outside the States. Which is a pity, for many people whose opinions are worth respecting still hold to the view that Fred dancing with Barrie Chase was as good if not better than him dancing with Ginger Rogers or Rita Hayworth or Cyd Charisse.

A 60-year-old man dancing with a 22-year-old woman may sound a little absurd but it most certainly wasn't.

The only real chance moviegoers have had to judge Miss Chase's dancing ability occurred in that multi-million dollar all-star comedy *It's A Mad, Mad, Mad, Mad World*. Fred wasn't in it but just about everyone else was. Somewhere in the middle of the film, a scantily clad Barrie Chase jives with Dick Shawn. She dances sensuously and very moodily. She says hardly a word. But she doesn't have to. Her dancing speaks volumes.

But if the TV Fred Astaire of the 1960s and 1970s is now for most people only a memory, at least the screen Fred Astaire remains. Fred made the films not because they were anything special or outstanding (he never again received as good a role as the scientist in *On The Beach*) but more to keep his hand in and remain part of the contemporary movie scene.

The films were spread evenly over the two

Opposite bottom: *Fred
discards his dancing shoes
for the thrills of motor
racing in* On The Beach
(United Artists, 1959).

167

decades. In 1961 he appeared for Paramount in the comedy *The Pleasure Of His Company*, adapted by Samuel Taylor from his own stage play. It was an entertaining bauble of a movie, set in San Francisco with Fred as a charming, debonair playboy father who, without warning and after an absence of 15 years, abruptly reappears for his daughter's wedding. The story was slight and, for the most part, the film was exposed for what it was, a filmed stage play. But Fred's old sparkle, grace and charm were still evident even though the only occasion he danced in the film (along with others on a routine dance floor) was with Debbie Reynolds who played his daughter. His other co-star was Lilli Palmer, wonderfully stylish as his former wife.

A year later he returned to Columbia, the scene of his old movies with Rita Hayworth. Harry Cohn and Rita and most of the Columbia stalwarts he had known in the old days were long since gone but at least two of the stars who had made their names under the Columbia banner were still working on the lot – the young Jack Lemmon and Kim Novak, both of whom had started at the studio in the mid-1950s.

The film was called *The Notorious Landlady*. Directed by Richard Quine and part scripted by Blake Edwards, it belongs in that relatively rare genre of films, the comedy-mystery thriller. Set in a foggy London (but shot in Hollywood), the picture involves a lovesick American diplomat with a silky blonde murder suspect and adds, as extra ingredients, dark alleys, poisoned kidney pies, lethal matrons and a desperate climactic chase along the rocky cliffs of Penzance. The dialogue was sharp and witty. Lemmon played the diplomat, Novak the murder suspect. Fred played Lemmon's boss Franklyn Ambruster and more than held his own in the stylish romp. 'A comedy of murder' perhaps best sums up *The Notorious Landlady*. Edith Oliver in *The New Yorker* described it as 'a picture that is entertaining and exciting, often simultaneously'. She added: 'I don't see how anyone could help but have a good time watching it.'

In 1968 Fred made his first movie on the Warner Brothers Burbank lot. It was one of the few major studios at which he hadn't worked. The film was the whimsical musical *Finian's Rainbow*.

He played a wizened old character called Finian McLonergan who journeys to Fort Knox with a crock of gold he has stolen from a leprechaun. His theory is that if he buries his gold near Fort Knox it will grow and multiply just like the federal reserves. A subplot has a racist senator of the area being turned black so that he can experience for himself what it feels like to be a victim of bigotry.

Finian's Rainbow is a blend of satire, blarney and social comment. Its message is that the real riches of life lie not in gold but in warm, goodhearted people. It was the last of the great postwar Broadway musicals to reach the screen. The delay was primarily because producers felt that its content was too controversial for the 1950s and early 1960s.

Fred looked very different from the elegant man about town of his 1930s films. He appeared mostly with a two-day stubble of beard, wore an old cardigan with fraying elbows and also shirts with threadbare cuffs. But with his old friend Hermes Pan back on the set as dance director he moved as nimbly as ever.

Petula Clark (as Finian's daughter) and the ebullient young Tommy Steele (as the leprechaun) co-starred with Fred. Between them they shared some of the loveliest songs (all of them composed

Father of the bride! Fred with Debbie Reynolds, Tab Hunter, Lilli Palmer, Gary Merrill and Charles Ruggles in The Pleasure Of His Company *(Paramount, 1961).*

Above: The Notorious Landlady *(Columbia, 1962). Fred with co-star Jack Lemmon.*

Opposite: *Fred as the Irish immigrant Finian McLonergan who journeys to Fort Knox with a crock of gold stolen from a leprechaun. The film – the 1968 Warner musical* Finian's Rainbow.

by Burton Lane and Yip Harburg) of the postwar era – 'How Are Things In Glocca Morra?', 'Old Devil Moon', 'When The Idle Poor Become The Idle Rich' and 'This Time Of Year'.

The critical reaction to *Finian's Rainbow* was mostly unfavourable (the film was one of the first to be directed by the young Francis Ford Coppola) but over the years its reputation has grown and it now belongs with the more imaginative musicals of the era. During shooting Fred – a non-smoker and a light drinker – celebrated his 68th birthday and revealed that he had no secrets about keeping himself fit: 'I don't do any workouts. I don't like exercises; what I call physical torture or bends at the bar in ballet. I do my own exercises when I am about to perform in a dance. I just work into it until I get feeling perfectly loose and keep my balance the way I want it and have control of the floor – like the track in other words, the running track.'

He also said: 'The idea of *just* dancing doesn't excite me any longer. Something has to excite me, capture my imagination. But when the old inspiration strikes and the rhythm moves, I dance better than I ever did.'

One time the inspiration *did* strike was when he did a two-and-a-half-minute dance routine on the

Hollywood Palace television show. It took him four weeks to get the dance exactly as he wanted it. 'Getting started on a routine is tough,' he said, 'but the big secret is knowing when to stop. A few seconds too long can kill a number dead. And that's how I feel about my career now. It'd be kinda tragic if I tried to stay around too long and people started saying "Well, gee whiz, he's not as good as he used to be". Every time I perform I watch for that. The first ragged routine and it'll be too late – I won't have quit fast enough.'

In his next film, the comedy caper thriller *Midas Run* (1969), Fred found himself still preoccupied with gold, this time as a veteran British secret service officer who, annoyed that he has been passed over for a knighthood, turns crooked. He gets back at the establishment by hijacking a gold shipment worth $15 million. The film, which co-starred Richard Crenna, was a pleasant enough diversion with Fred and Anne Heywood seeing it through.

The film that really began 'Astaire time' all over again, however, was a movie that was made in the mid-1970s, and its success was totally unexpected. Made is perhaps not the correct term, compiled is nearer the mark. The film was *That's Entertainment* and it was the dream child of Jack Haley Jr, son of

Fred with Barbara Hancock in the 1968 Warner Bros musical Finian's Rainbow.

the actor who played the Tin Man in the classic *The Wizard Of Oz.*

The story behind its production is an interesting one because it revealed that although Fred and other musical stars of his era had long since vanished from the scene, there was still a demand to see his inimitable form of song and dance, especially from youngsters who had previously seen snatches of his films only on television and never on the big cinema screen.

At first Haley found it difficult to convince the

MGM executives that the public would want to see stars such as Fred, Gene Kelly, Judy Garland and others in a compilation of musical clips from their best films. The best he could get out of them was a promise that they would look at things more closely if he put together a short piece of film showing some of the clips he had in mind and linking them so they made sense to a contemporary audience. It took Haley six months, with practically no staff, to get something together. He got so carried away that when he'd finished compiling his so-called

Fred, aged 69 but still going solo in Finian's Rainbow *(Warner Bros, 1968).*

Two not-so-civil servants, nose to nose! Fred with Ralph Richardson in the 1969 thriller Midas Run *(Selmur Pictures)*

short film it ran for 90 minutes.

When Haley showed it to the MGM executives they couldn't take their eyes off the screen. When it was over they turned to him and said: 'Why didn't you show us more?' They hadn't realised they had been watching the screen for an hour and a half. Haley was given the go-ahead and *That's Entertainment* was born.

To introduce the different sequences he selected 11 top stars, all of whom had worked regularly at MGM during their careers. Elizabeth Taylor introduced one section, Liza Minnelli another, Frank Sinatra another. James Stewart, Peter Lawford and Mickey Rooney also served as narrator-hosts. As, of course, did Gene Kelly and eventually Fred; although because of Fred's dislike for nostalgia and looking back into the past it took Jack Haley a bit of time to talk him into taking part.

Jack Haley selected all the material for the film. In the sequence devoted to Fred at MGM he included 'They Can't Take That Away From Me' and 'Shoes With Wings On' from *The Barkleys Of Broadway*; 'Sunday Jumps' and 'You're All The World To Me' from *Royal Wedding*; and 'Dancing In The Dark', 'By Myself' and 'I Guess I'll Have To Change My Plan' from *The Band Wagon*.

Haley never got any feedback on whether Fred agreed with his selections. In fact he had a feeling that Fred was too embarrassed to make any comments. The same thing applied to Gene Kelly. Haley did his best to find out whether they

approved of his selections but he couldn't get anything out of either of them.

He quickly found, however, that Fred was just as much a perfectionist as ever. The 75-year-old star insisted on re-recording his voice 12 times for his little narration spot and even then he wasn't satisfied.

Remembers Haley today: 'Fred would think of something else he wanted to say about Gene Kelly so he'd come back to the studio for another "take". In the end I had to say "Fred, this film has *got* to get out to the theatres soon, you can't keep changing the narration". Fred would say, "Yes Jack, I know, just let me try one more thing".'

'I think he and Gene were pleased with the result. If they were displeased they never in any way, shape or form, let me know about it and boy did I try to find out. But it was like banging your head against a brick wall with both of them.'

There was no doubt that both Fred and Gene *did* find *That's Entertainment* a satisfying experience for two years later they agreed to feature as co-hosts on the sequel *That's Entertainment Part II*.

MGM veteran Saul Chaplin worked as associate producer on the second film. He was the one who approached the two stars, through their respective agents, about co-hosting the movie. 'Gene agreed to do it,' says Chaplin. 'Then Fred said, all right, he would do it but only, and his agent made a big point of this, providing there was no dancing. I said "OK, absolutely no dancing" and the contracts were signed.

'Well, I had written some lyrics for a song in the early part of the film that Fred and Gene were going to do. At our first rehearsal they started to learn the lyrics. At one point Fred said: "Gene, don't you think we can do 16 bars of dancing here?" I just sat at the piano and stared straight ahead, hoping against hope that he wouldn't change his mind. And he didn't. In the film there are three or four scenes where they dance. And it was Fred's suggestion.'

In the second film Chaplin and his co-producer Daniel Melnick included Fred performing with Cyd Charisse to 'All Of You' from *Silk Stockings*, dancing 'I Wanna Be A Dancin' Man' from *The Belle Of New York*, singing 'A Couple Of Swells' with Judy Garland in *Easter Parade*, performing 'Steppin' Out With My Baby' in the same film and singing 'Three Little Words' with Red Skelton.

The fact that the two *That's Entertainment* films proved to be such huge box-office successes both surprised and delighted MGM (and probably Fred and all the other stars too). The studio had obviously hoped to make a profit on the venture. $5 million profit would have been reasonable, $8 million to $10 million excellent. But when the first film went on to make $40 million they were astounded. *That's Entertainment* became the ninth highest grossing movie in the studio's history. It has since become one of the top selling video cassettes and has been the first tape to be entered into Hollywood's Hall of Fame.

Jack Haley had expected *That's Entertainment* to do well in the big cities where many film and musical buffs lived. What surprised him was that it did well all over the States, indeed all over the world, and that the queues around the blocks

. . . and even sharing a step or two with Gene as they revive the great days of MGM, That's Entertainment Part II *(1976)*.

artist be a dramatic or comedy performer or a musical one. Somehow Fred seems to have always been around. 'Always' equates with over 50 years in the movies, which is a largish chunk of the sound era. He has lightened many a grey, dismal day for people who have scurried into a cinema out of the rain and cheered those who have tried to forget the troubles of the world for a couple of hours. And he has done so with a pair of twinkling feet that have no equal. He has interpreted every dance from the fox-trot to jitterbug and rock'n'roll and he has done so in a medium that has allowed him to control the mechanics of his art and dazzle us with his dance magic. He has explored the whole scope of the dance. He has vented his anger against chairs and hatstands and he has expressed himself through a lyrical embrace, a jaunty stroll or simply a walk. His world has been one of chairs, tables, walls, ceilings, bars, ballrooms and bandstands. And it is a world which we have all enjoyed to the full along with him.

In recent times he has often popped up in the most unlikely films. In *The Towering Inferno* (1974) for instance he played a con man (a performance for which he received an Oscar nomination) and was one of those caught up in the raging fire that sweeps through the world's tallest skyscraper. And in the made-for-TV movie *The Man In The Santa Claus Suit* he played a cabby, a New York cop, a jeweller, a floorwalker, a hot dog stand owner, even Santa Claus himself. He even appeared in the horror film *Ghost Story* (1981), an x-certificate movie full of spooks and vengeful females and rotting flesh.

He has also got married again, in June 1980, to a woman under half his age (she was 35, he was 81) named Robyn Smith. A former jockey – Fred first met her during one of his many visits to the race-track – Robyn has lived happily with Fred at his Hollywood home ever since.

When interviewed in recent years, Fred, shy and diffident as always, has continued to stress his preference for living in the present and not remembering the past. And he remains as self-deprecating as ever about his talents. His voice, for instance, the one for which so many composers wrote great songs for. His opinion of that?

'Lousy! Well, not too bad I suppose. I'm not a particular fan of my own singing voice. I think the main reason I can be satisfied with it is that composers have liked the way I do their songs. But I'd have been broke if I had tried to be a singer alone.'

As for his movies? His reaction to those usually depends on Fred's mood. On one occasion he referred to them as 'kinda stupid. Very trite boy and girl plots with no depth. There was never any depth to anything we did. The stories were just stupid.' On another occasion he said: 'I see them on television once in a while, and you know, they are pretty darned good. I saw one not too long ago and turned on in the middle of it. For the life of me I couldn't remember what it was all about so I had to stay to the end to see what happened. And there was

Fred with Ginger Rogers at the That's Entertainment *celebrations in Hollywood.*

weren't just made up of people who remembered the musicals from the old days, but also teenagers. As he drove home from the studio he used to pass a cinema and noticed that although the queues were at first made up of middle-aged people, they gradually began to be joined by college kids and were then made up entirely of college kids.

Says Haley: 'I think my father said it best. He said film is timeless. He said if you take Fred Astaire and Eleanor Powell dancing to "Begin The Beguine" it's not dated. Excellence doesn't date and that's an excellent number. People respond to excellence. They know that's good dancing, they know that's good music. So what if it is in black and white and it's 40 years old. It doesn't matter. It's exciting and people appreciate it.'

There's certainly no doubt that audiences have appreciated Fred Astaire over the years, perhaps more than any other screen artist, whether that

a pretty good routine in there. I was pleased with that. In fact it looked so darned good I wondered how I ever did it!'

As for ambitions unfulfilled? Very few. At golf he's achieved a hole in one so he can't better things in that direction. His love of horses was rewarded with the achievements of his beloved Triplicate but he has never won the Kentucky Derby or the Epsom Derby with one of his horses. 'I don't care so much about the Kentucky Derby,' he once said. 'I've won some good races. But Epsom would be fun to win.'

His only major disappointment has been that he has never managed to write a complete score for a Broadway show: 'I'm a frustrated songwriter,' he says, 'and I would like to have written a musical comedy score. But that's just about the only thing I didn't get done.'

But even though he didn't write his musical comedy, Fred did at least manage to achieve half his ambition. For a dozen or so years in the late 1920s and early 1930s he wrote many songs. His best known number and one that went straight into the hit parade, remains 'I'm Building Up To An Awful Letdown' which had lyrics by Johnny Mercer. Others written by Fred during the period included 'Tappin' The Time', 'More And More', 'Hello Baby', 'Just Like Taking Candy From A Baby', 'Not My Girl' and in 1936, 'Just One More Dance, Madame' (lyrics by Dave Dreyer

and Paul Francis Webster) and 'I'll Never Let You Go' (lyrics by Dreyer and Jack Ellis).

In fact, so talented was Fred as a songwriter that if he had ever decided to retire he might well have turned out to be one of the most successful writers of popular songs.

To bid farewell to Fred Astaire is difficult. How indeed does one say goodbye to a man whom Irving Berlin described as having 'raised tap dancing to an elegant art' and who was once described by novelist John O'Hara as 'the living symbol of all that is best in showbusiness?'

To leave him quietly at his Hollywood home with his wife, his piano, his pool table, his trophies and awards doesn't seem quite right somehow. Hollywood itself luckily comes to the rescue. Just about all Fred's great musicals build up to a spectacular climax and three or four years ago Hollywood itself staged such a climax for Fred. The date was 10 April 1981. The occasion – when Fred became the ninth recipient (Gene Kelly was honoured in 1985) of the American Film Institute's Life Achievement Award.

It was a glittering occasion of the kind only Hollywood could stage. The venue was the plush Beverly Hilton hotel off Wilshire Boulevard. On hand in the crowded ballroom were stars who had worked with Fred for years and friends who had known him for even longer. At the head table he was joined by his wife Robyn, his daughter Ava

Fred earns his only Oscar nomination – for his performance as the confidence trickster who manages to survive the all-consuming fire that strikes at the world's tallest skyscraper The Towering Inferno *(Twentieth Century-Fox/ Warner Bros, 1974).*

and her husband, his son Fred and his wife, and his old pal Hermes Pan. Only two people were missing from Fred's night of triumph – his beloved mother Ann who had died six years earlier at the remarkable age of 96 and his sister Adele who died that very year, aged 84.

Anyone who was anyone was there, 2000 all told, each paying $300 a head. In short, it was the kind of occasion that Fred had succeeded in ducking in all his years in Hollywood. But on that night of 10 April he knew he had no option. His graciousness and humility overcame his natural reserve and, even if he did feel the strain of the occasion, he never once let it show. In fact, he cut more of a dashing figure than any of the other tuxedoed men in the room for around his waist he wore a startling pink sash.

Whether or not Fred enjoyed the dinner that preceded the event can only be guessed at. Probably not. He would have been too nervous at what was to come in the way of tributes. And at 9.05 pm, those tributes began as one after the other, in a two-hour spectacular, Hollywood's

Above: *Last dance. Fred's last screen dancing partner! Jennifer Jones shares a waltz in the all-star disaster movie* The Towering Inferno *(Twentieth Century-Fox/ Warner Bros, 1974).*

Right: *Fred as a New York cop, one of the several roles he played in the TV movie* The Man In The Santa Claus Suit *(1983).*

greatest celebrities came on stage to talk affectionately of the man who had entertained the world so regally. Some recalled how he had worked them till their feet ached but had earned them a place in movie history as one of the lucky few dancing partners of Fred Astaire.

Produced by George Stevens Jr who referred to Fred as 'the old so-and-so from Omaha who became the greatest musical performer in the history of motion pictures', the show was emceed by Fred's long-time friend David Niven who flew in from Switzerland for the occasion. He began by showing Fred in a scene from *Top Hat* and then introduced a brilliantly compiled series of montages of Fred's greatest screen dances. Even that distinguished and knowledgeable audience gasped in admiration as 50 years of brilliance unfolded on the screen.

James Cagney, who was one of the stars on hand, said simply: 'Fred Astaire was the greatest dancer I've ever seen in my life'. Ginger Rogers, who had starred with Fred in more pictures than any other star but was tied up in a show and couldn't be present, sent a congratulatory telegram. So too did President Reagan.

Eleanor Powell came on stage to recall how she had stepped in as Ginger's first replacement. Audrey Hepburn and Cyd Charisse both came forward with their own special tributes and memories. As did, to the delight of many, Barrie Chase. She recalled how Fred had repeatedly peeked into her rehearsal hall before selecting her and stressed what a hard taskmaster he was. 'Dancing with Fred Astaire was tough', she said,

then added, as she turned to Fred, 'there were times you were a monster. And I wish I could start it all over again.'

Director/choreographer Bob Fosse recalled how he had idolised Fred as a dancer at MGM and mentioned: 'What always impressed me about Fred was his tremendous desire for perfection.'

Mikhail Baryshnikov made one of the most amusing speeches of the night. He said: 'I have been invited to say something about how dancers feel about Fred Astaire. It's no secret we hate him. He gives us complexes because he's too perfect His perfection is an absurdity, it's hard to face.'

Gene Kelly was left to sum up everyone's feelings when he said: 'Fifty years from now the only one of today's dancers who will be remembered will be Fred Astaire.'

As Fred got up to reply to all the tributes it was probably one of the most nerve-racking moments of his life. Of the honour of receiving the Life Achievement Award, he said: 'I'm thrilled to death. I can't explain it any more than that, I really can't.' He added jokingly: 'If I had a little thing I could squirt in my eye, I could cry. I really mean it.'

And then with disarming honesty and for once talking entirely seriously about his work he looked around at the crowded gathering and explained all the 75 years of blood, sweat and tears with these words: 'All the dances in the film clips shown tonight looked good to me. When you do a movie – and I know Gene Kelly will agree with me – you're sometimes a little disappointed in what you're doing. But tonight I'm proud. I'm proud that it still hangs on!'

Opposite: *The ultimate triumph! A career saluted by the American Film Institute. Fred with his Life Achievement Award presented to him at the Beverly Hilton in Hollywood in 1981.*

Right: *Fred with his second wife Robyn.*

Below: *Fred with his wife Robyn and Gene Kelly with his daughter Bridget at the American Film Institute Life Achievement Award ceremony in Hollywood.*

FILMOGRAPHY

Dancing Lady 1933. Metro-Goldwyn-Mayer. Director: Robert Z. Leonard. Producer: David O. Selznick. Lyrics: Harold Adamson, Dorothy Fields, Lorenz Hart, Arthur Freed. Music: Burton Lane, Jimmy McHugh, Richard Rodgers, Nacio Herb Brown. Musical numbers: 'Hey, Young Fella', 'Hold Your Man', 'Everything I Have Is Yours', 'My Dancing Lady', 'Heigh-Ho, The Gang's All Here', 'Let's Go Bavarian', 'That's The Rhythm Of The Day'. *Stars*: Joan Crawford, Clark Gable, Franchot Tone, Fred Astaire.

Flying Down To Rio 1933. RKO. Director: Thornton Freeland. Producer: Louis Brock. Lyrics: Edward Eliscu, Gus Kahn. Music: Vincent Youmans. Musical numbers: 'Music Makes Me', 'The Carioca', 'Orchids In The Moonlight', 'Flying Down To Rio'. *Stars*: Dolores Del Rio, Gene Raymond, Raul Roulien, Ginger Rogers, Fred Astaire, Eric Blore.

The Gay Divorcee (UK: The Gay Divorce) 1934. RKO. Director: Mark Sandrich. Producer: Pandro S. Berman. Lyrics: Cole Porter, Herb Magidson, Mack Gordon. Music: Cole Porter, Con Conrad, Harry Revel. Musical numbers: 'Don't Let It Bother You', 'Needle In A Haystack', 'Let's K-nock K-nees', 'Night And Day', 'The Continental'. *Stars*: Fred Astaire, Ginger Rogers, Alice Brady, Edward Everett Horton, Erik Rhodes, Eric Blore.

Roberta 1935. RKO. Director: William A. Seiter. Producer: Pandro S. Berman. Lyrics: Otto Harbach, Dorothy Fields, Ballard Macdonald, Bernard Dougall. Music: Jerome Kern, James F. Hanley, Oscar Hammerstein II. Musical numbers: 'Indiana', 'Let's Begin', 'Russian song' (traditional), 'I'll Be Hard To Handle', 'Yesterdays', 'I Won't Dance', 'Smoke Gets In Your Eyes', 'Lovely To Look At'. *Stars*: Irene Dunne, Fred Astaire, Ginger Rogers, Randolph Scott, Helen Westley.

Top Hat 1935. RKO. Director: Mark Sandrich. Producer: Pandro S. Berman. Lyrics and music: Irving Berlin. Musical numbers: 'No Strings', 'Isn't This A Lovely Day?', 'Top Hat, White Tie And Tails', 'Cheek To Cheek', 'The Piccolino'. *Stars*: Fred Astaire, Ginger Rogers, Edward Everett Horton, Helen Broderick, Erik Rhodes, Eric Blore.

Follow The Fleet 1936. RKO. Director: Mark Sandrich. Producer: Pandro S. Berman. Lyrics and music: Irving Berlin. Musical numbers: 'We Saw The Sea', 'Let Yourself Go', 'Get Thee Behind Me Satan', 'I'd Rather Lead A Band', 'But Where Are You?', 'I'm Putting All My Eggs In One Basket', 'Let's Face The Music And Dance'. *Stars*: Fred Astaire, Ginger Rogers, Randolph Scott, Harriet Hilliard.

Swing Time 1936. RKO. Director: George Stevens. Producer: Pandro S. Berman. Lyrics: Dorothy Fields. Music: Jerome Kern. Musical numbers: 'It's Not In The Cards', 'Pick Yourself Up', 'The Way You Look Tonight', 'Waltz In Swing Time', 'A Fine Romance', 'Bojangles Of Harlem', 'Never Gonna Dance'. *Stars*: Fred Astaire, Ginger Rogers, Victor Moore, Helen Broderick, Eric Blore, Betty Furness, Georges Metaxa.

Shall We Dance? 1937. RKO. Director: Mark Sandrich. Producer: Pandro S. Berman. Lyrics: Ira Gershwin. Music: George Gershwin. Musical numbers: 'Beginners' Luck', 'Slap That Bass', 'Walking The Dog', 'They All Laughed', 'Let's Call The Whole Thing Off', 'They Can't Take That Away From Me', 'Shall We Dance?'. *Stars*: Fred Astaire, Ginger Rogers, Edward Everett Horton, Eric Blore, Harriet Hoctor.

A Damsel In Distress 1937. RKO. Director: George Stevens. Producer: Pandro S. Berman. Lyrics: Ira Gershwin. Music: George Gershwin. Musical numbers: 'I Can't Be Bothered Now', 'The Jolly Tar And The Milkmaid', 'Put Me To The Test', 'Stiff Upper Lip', 'Sing Of Spring', 'Things Are Looking Up', 'A Foggy Day', 'Nice Work If You Can Get It'. *Stars*: Fred Astaire, George Burns, Gracie Allen, Joan Fontaine, Reginald Gardiner, Constance Collier.

Carefree 1938. RKO. Director: Mark Sandrich. Producer: Pandro S. Berman. Lyrics and music: Irving Berlin. Musical numbers: 'Since They Turned Loch Lomond Into Swing', 'The Night Is Filled With Music', 'I Used To Be Colour Blind', 'The Yam', 'Change Partners'. *Stars*: Fred Astaire, Ginger Rogers, Ralph Bellamy.

The Story Of Vernon And Irene Castle 1939. RKO. Director: H. C. Potter. Producers: Pandro S. Berman, George Haight. Musical numbers: 'Only When You're In My Arms' (Conrad, Kalmar and Ruby), 'Waiting for the Robert E. Lee', 'Too Much Mustard' (Castle Walk), 'Rose Room' (Castle Tango), 'Little Brown Jug' (Castle Polka), 'Dengozo' (Maxixe), 'When They Were Dancing Around', 'Pretty Baby' (Très Jolie), 'Millicent Waltz', 'Night Of Gladness', 'Missouri Waltz', 'By The Light Of The Silvery Moon', 'Who's Your Lady Friend?', 'Yama Yama Man', 'Oh, You Beautiful Doll', 'Glow-Worm', 'By The Beautiful Sea', 'Row, Row, Row', 'Come, Josephine In My Flying Machine', 'Cuddle Up A Little Closer', 'You're Here And I'm Here', 'Chicago', 'Hello, Frisco, Hello', 'Way Down Yonder In New Orleans', 'Take Me Back To New York Town', 'It's A Long Way To Tipperary', 'Keep The Home Fires Burning', 'Smiles', 'The Darktown Strutters' Ball', 'Over There'. *Stars*: Fred Astaire, Ginger Rogers, Edna May Oliver, Walter Brennan, Lew Fields.

Broadway Melody Of 1940 1940. Metro-Goldwyn-Mayer. Director: Norman Taurog. Producer: Jack Cummings. Lyrics and music: Cole Porter. Musical numbers: 'Please Don't Monkey With Broadway', 'I Am The Captain', 'Between You And Me', 'I've Got My Eyes On You', 'Juke Box Dance', 'I Concentrate On You', 'Begin The Beguine'. *Stars*: Fred Astaire, Eleanor Powell, George Murphy, Frank Morgan, Ian Hunter.

Second Chorus 1940. Paramount. Director: H. C. Potter. Producer: Boris Morros. Lyrics: Johnny Mercer, Will Harris, E. Y. Harburg. Music: Artie Shaw, Bernard Hanighen, Hal Borne, Victor Young, Johnny Green. Musical numbers: 'I Ain't Hep To That Step But I'll Dig It', 'Sweet Sue', 'Love Of My Life', 'I'm Yours', 'Concerto For Clarinet', 'Poor Mr Chisholm'. *Stars*: Fred Astaire, Paulette

Goddard, Artie Shaw, Burgess Meredith, Charles Butterworth.

You'll Never Get Rich 1941. Columbia. Director: Sidney Lanfield. Producer: Samuel Bischoff. Lyrics and music: Cole Porter. Musical numbers: 'Boogie Woogie Barcarolle', 'Dream Dancing', 'Shootin' The Works For Uncle Sam', 'Since I Kissed My Baby Goodbye', 'A-stairable Rag', 'So Near And Yet So Far', 'Wedding Cake Walk'. *Stars*: Fred Astaire, Rita Hayworth, Robert Benchley.

Holiday Inn 1942. Paramount. Director: Mark Sandrich. Producer: Mark Sandrich. Lyrics and music: Irving Berlin. Musical numbers: 'I'll Capture Your Heart Singing', 'Lazy', 'You're Easy To Dance With', 'White Christmas', 'Happy Holiday', 'Holiday Inn', 'Let's Start The New Year Right', 'Abraham', 'Be Careful, It's My Heart', 'I Can't Tell A Lie', 'Easter Parade', 'Let's Say It With Firecrackers', 'Song Of Freedom', 'Plenty To Be Thankful For', 'Oh, How I Hate To Get Up In The Morning'. *Stars*: Bing Crosby, Fred Astaire, Marjorie Reynolds, Virginia Dale.

You Were Never Lovelier 1942. Columbia. Director: William A. Seiter. Producer: Louis F. Edelman. Lyrics: Johnny Mercer. Music: Jerome Kern. Musical numbers: 'Chiu Chiu (Niconar Molinare)', 'Dearly Beloved', 'Audition Dance', 'I'm Old-fashioned', 'The Shorty George', 'Wedding In The Spring', 'You Were Never Lovelier', 'These Orchids'. *Stars*: Fred Astaire, Rita Hayworth, Adolphe Menjou, Xavier Cugat.

The Sky's The Limit 1943. RKO. Director: Edward H. Griffith. Producer: David Hempstead. Lyrics: Johnny Mercer, Bert Kalmar, Frank Loesser. Music: Harold Arlen, Harry Ruby, Jimmy McHugh. Musical numbers: 'My Shining Hour', 'A Lot In Common With You', 'One For My Baby', 'Three Little Words', 'Can't Get Out Of This Mood', 'I Get The Neck Of The Chicken'. *Stars*: Fred Astaire, Joan Leslie, Robert Benchley, Robert Ryan, Eric Blore.

Ziegfeld Follies 1945. Metro-Goldwyn-Mayer. Director: Vincente Minnelli. Producer: Arthur Freed. Musical numbers: 'It's Delightful To Be Married', 'I'm An Indian', 'If You Knew Suzie', 'Bring On The Beautiful Girls', 'Bring On The Wonderful Men', 'Libiamo Ne' Licti Calici', 'This Heart Of Mine', 'Love', 'Limehouse Blues', 'Wot Cher', 'Madame Crematon', 'The Babbitt And The Bromide', 'There's Beauty Everywhere'. *Stars*: Fred Astaire, Lucille Ball, Lucille Bremer, Fanny Brice, Judy Garland, Kathryn Grayson, Lena Horne, Gene Kelly, Red Skelton, Esther Williams, William Powell. Technicolor.

Yolanda And The Thief 1945. Metro-Goldwyn-Mayer. Director: Vincente Minnelli. Producer: Arthur Freed. Lyrics: Arthur Freed. Music: Harry Warren. Musical numbers: 'This Is A Day For Love', 'Angel', 'Will You Marry Me?', 'Yolanda', 'Coffee Time'. *Stars*: Fred Astaire, Lucille Bremer, Frank Morgan. Technicolor.

Blue Skies 1946. Paramount. Director: Stuart Heisler. Producer: Sol. C. Siegel. Lyrics and music: Irving Berlin. Musical numbers: 'A Pretty Girl Is Like A Melody', 'I've Got My Captain Working For Me Now', 'You'd Be Surprised', 'All By Myself', 'Serenade To An Old-fashioned Girl', 'Puttin' On The Ritz', 'C-U-B-A', 'A Couple Of Song And Dance Men', 'You Keep Coming Back Like A Song', 'Always', 'Blue Skies', 'The Little Things In Life', 'Not For All The Rice In China', 'Russian Lullaby', 'Everybody Step', 'How Deep Is The Ocean?', 'Getting Nowhere', 'Heat Wave', 'Any Bonds Today?', 'This Is The Army, Mr Jones', 'White Christmas', 'Tell Me, Little Gypsy', 'Nobody Knows', 'Mandy', 'Some Sunny Day', 'When You Walked Out', 'Because I Love You', 'How Many Times?', 'Lazy', 'The Song Is Ended'. *Stars*: Bing Crosby, Fred Astaire, Joan Caulfield, Billy DeWolfe, Olga San Juan. Technicolor.

Easter Parade 1948. Metro-Goldwyn-Mayer. Director: Charles Walters. Producer: Arthur Freed. Lyrics and music: Irving Berlin. Musical numbers: 'Happy Easter', 'Drum Crazy', 'It Only Happens When I Dance With You', 'Everybody's Doin' It', 'I Want To Go Back To Michigan', 'Beautiful Faces Need Beautiful Clothes', 'A Fella With An Umbrella', 'I Love A Piano', 'Snooky Ookums', 'Ragtime Violin', 'When The Midnight Choo-Choo Leaves For Alabam', 'Shakin' The Blues Away', 'Steppin' Out With My Baby', 'A Couple Of Swells', 'The Girl On The Magazine Cover', 'Better Luck Next Time', 'Easter Parade', 'At The Devil's Ball', 'This Is The Life', 'Along Came Ruth', 'Call Me Up Some Rainy Afternoon'. *Stars*: Judy Garland, Fred Astaire, Peter Lawford, Ann Miller. Technicolor.

The Barkleys Of Broadway 1949. Metro-Goldwyn-Mayer. Director: Charles Walters. Producer: Arthur Freed. Lyrics: Ira Gershwin, Arthur Freed. Music: Harry Warren. Musical numbers: 'Swing Trot', 'You'd Be So Hard To Replace', 'Bouncin' The Blues', 'My One And Only Highland Fling', 'A Weekend In The Country', 'Shoes With Wings On', 'They Can't Take That Away From Me' (George Gershwin), 'Manhattan Downbeat'. *Stars*: Fred Astaire, Ginger Rogers, Oscar Levant. Technicolor.

Three Little Words 1950. Metro-Goldwyn-Mayer. Director: Richard Thorpe. Producer: Jack Cummings. Lyrics: Bert Kalmar, Edgar Leslie, Arthur Freed. Music: Harry Ruby, Herman Ruby, Ted Snyder, Harry Puck, Herbert Stothart, Nacio Herb Brown. Musical numbers: 'Where Did You Get That Girl?', 'She's Mine, All Mine', 'Mr and Mrs Hoofer At Home', 'My Sunny Tennessee', 'So Long Oo long', 'Who's Sorry Now?', 'Come On Papa', 'Nevertheless', 'All Alone Monday', 'You Smiled At Me', 'I Wanna Be Loved By You', 'Up In The Clouds', 'Thinking Of You', 'Hooray For Captain Spaulding', 'I Love You So Much', 'You Are My Lucky Star', 'Three Little Words'. *Stars*: Fred Astaire, Red Skelton, Vera-Ellen, Arlene Dahl, Keenan Wynn, Debbie Reynolds. Technicolor.

Let's Dance 1950. Paramount. Director: Norman Z. McLeod. Producer: Robert Fellows. Lyrics and music: Frank Loesser. Musical numbers: 'Can't Stop Talking', 'Piano Dance', 'Jack And The Beanstalk', 'Oh, Them Dudes', 'Why Fight The Feeling?', 'The Hyacinth', 'Tunnel Of Love'. *Stars*: Betty Hutton, Fred Astaire, Roland Young, Ruth Warrick, Lucile Watson. Technicolor.

Royal Wedding (UK: Wedding Bells) 1951. Metro-Goldwyn-Mayer. Director: Stanley Donen. Producer: Arthur Freed. Lyrics: Alan Jay Lerner. Music: Burton Lane. Musical numbers: 'Ev'ry Night At Seven', 'Sunday Jumps', 'Open Your Eyes', 'The Happiest Day Of My Life', 'How Could You Believe Me When I Said I Love You When You Know I've Been A Liar All My Life?', 'Too Late Now', 'You're All

The World To Me', 'I Left My Hat In Haiti', 'What A Lovely Day For A Wedding'. *Stars*: Fred Astaire, Jane Powell, Peter Lawford, Sarah Churchill, Keenan Wynn. Technicolor.

The Belle Of New York 1952. Metro-Goldwyn-Mayer. Director: Charles Walters. Producer: Arthur Freed. Lyrics: Johnny Mercer. Music: Harry Warren. Musical numbers: 'When I'm Out With The Belle Of New York', 'Bachelor Dinner Song', 'Let A Little Love Come In' (Roger Edens), 'Seeing's Believing', 'Baby Doll', 'Oops', 'A Bride's Wedding Day', 'Naughty But Nice', 'I Wanna Be A Dancin' Man', 'Thank You Mr Currier, Thank You Mr Ives'. *Stars*: Fred Astaire, Vera-Ellen, Marjorie Main, Keenan Wynn, Alice Pearce. Technicolor.

The Band Wagon 1953. Metro-Goldwyn-Mayer. Director: Vincente Minnelli. Producer: Arthur Freed. Lyrics: Howard Dietz. Music: Arthur Schwartz. Musical numbers: 'By Myself', 'A Shine On Your Shoes', 'That's Entertainment', 'Beggar Waltz' (from *Giselle*), 'Dancing In The Dark', 'You And The Night And The Music', 'Something To Remember You By', 'High And Low', 'I Love Louisa', 'New Sun In The Sky', 'I Guess I'll Have To Change My Plan', 'Louisana Hayride', 'Triplets', 'Girl Hunt: A Murder Mystery in Jazz' (narrative, Alan Jay Lerner). *Stars*: Fred Astaire, Cyd Charisse, Oscar Levant, Nanette Fabray, Jack Buchanan. Technicolor.

Daddy Long Legs 1955. Twentieth Century-Fox. Director: Jean Negulesco. Producer: Samuel G. Engel. Lyrics and music: Johnny Mercer. Ballet music: Alex North. Musical numbers: 'History Of The Beat', 'C-A-T Spells Cat', 'Daddy Long Legs', 'Welcome Egghead', 'Daydream Sequence, (Texas Millionaire – International Playboy – Guardian Angel), 'Dream', 'Slue-foot', 'Something's Gotta Give', 'Dancing Through Life' ballet. *Stars*: Fred Astaire, Leslie Caron, Terry Moore, Thelma Ritter, Fred Clark. DeLuxe color, CinemaScope.

Funny Face 1957. Paramount. Director: Stanley Donen. Producer: Roger Edens. Lyrics: Ira Gershwin, Leonard Gershe. Music: George Gershwin, Roger Edens. Musical numbers: 'Think Pink', 'How Long Has This Been Going On?', 'Funny Face', 'Bonjour Paris', 'Basal Metabolism', 'Let's Kiss And Make Up', 'He Loves And She Loves', 'Oh, How To Be Lovely', 'Marche Funèbre', 'Clap Yo' Hands', 'S'Wonderful'. *Stars*: Audrey Hepburn, Fred Astaire, Kay Thompson, Michel Auclair. Technicolor.

Silk Stockings 1957. Metro-Goldwyn-Mayer. Director: Rouben Mamoulian. Producer: Arthur Freed. Lyrics and music: Cole Porter. Musical numbers: 'Too Bad', 'Paris Loves Lovers', 'Stereophonic Sound', 'It's A Chemical Reaction', 'That's All', 'All Of You', 'Satin And Silk', 'Silk Stockings', 'Without Love', 'Fated To Be Mated', 'Siberia', 'Josephine', 'The Red Blues', 'The Ritz Roll And Rock', 'I've Got You Under My Skin', 'Close', 'You'd Be So Nice To Come Home To', 'You Can Do No Wrong'. *Stars*: Fred Astaire, Cyd Charisse, Janis Paige, Peter Lorre, Jules Munshin, Joseph Buloff. Metrocolor, CinemaScope.

On The Beach 1959. United Artists. Director and producer: Stanley Kramer. *Stars*: Gregory Peck, Ava Gardner, Fred Astaire, Anthony Perkins, Donna Anderson.

The Pleasure Of His Company 1961. Paramount. Director: George Seaton. Producer: William Perlberg. *Stars*: Fred Astaire, Debbie Reynolds, Lilli Palmer, Tab Hunter, Gary Merrill. Technicolor.

The Notorious Lady 1962. Kohlmar-Quine Productions/Columbia. Director: Richard Quine. Producer: Fred Kohlmar. *Stars*: Kim Novak, Jack Lemmon, Fred Astaire, Lionel Jeffries, Estelle Winwood.

Finian's Rainbow 1968. Warner Brothers-Seven Arts. Director: Francis Ford Coppola. Producer: Joseph Landon. Lyrics: E. Y. Harburg. Music: Burton Lane. Musical numbers: 'This Time Of The Year', 'How Are Things In Glocca Morra?', 'Look To The Rainbow', 'If This Isn't Love', 'Something Sort Of Grandish', 'That Great Come-And-Get-It-Day', 'Old Devil Moon', 'When The Idle Poor Become The Idle Rich', 'When I'm Not Near The Girl I Love', 'Rain Dance', 'The Begat'. *Stars*: Fred Astaire, Petula Clark, Tommy Steele, Don Franscks, Keenan Wynn. Technicolor.

Midas Run (UK: A Run On Gold) 1969. Motion Pictures International-Selmur Pictures. Director: Alf Kjellin. Producer: Raymond Stross. *Stars*: Fred Astaire, Anne Heywood, Richard Crenna, Roddy McDowall, Ralph Richardson, Cesar Romero. Technicolor.

That's Entertainment 1974. Metro-Goldwyn-Mayer. Director and compiler: Jack Haley Jr. Producers: Jack Haley Jr, Daniel Melnick. A compilation of MGM musical clips, hosted by Fred Astaire, Bing Crosby, Gene Kelly, Peter Lawford, Liza Minnelli, Donald O'Connor, Debbie Reynolds, Mickey Rooney, Frank Sinatra, James Stewart, Elizabeth Taylor. Fred's musical numbers: 'Begin The Beguine', 'They Can't Take That Away From Me', 'Rhythm Of The Day', 'I Guess I'll Have To Change My Plan', 'Hat Rack Dance', 'Shoes With Wings On', 'You're All The World To Me', 'Dancing In The Dark', 'By Myself', 'Sunday Jumps', 'The Babbitt and The Bromide'. Metrocolor.

The Towering Inferno 1974. Twentieth Century-Fox/Warner Brothers. Director: John Guillermin. Producer: Irwin Allen. *Stars*: Steve McQueen, Paul Newman, William Holden, Faye Dunaway, Fred Astaire, Susan Blakely, Richard Chamberlain, Jennifer Jones, O. J. Simpson, Robert Vaughn, Robert Wagner. DeLuxe Color, Panavision.

That's Entertainment Part II 1976. Metro-Goldwyn-Mayer. Producers: Saul Chaplin, Daniel Melnick. Dance director: Gene Kelly. A second compilation of MGM musical clips, hosted by Fred Astaire and Gene Kelly. Fred's musical numbers: 'That's Entertainment', 'I Wanna Be A Dancin' Man', 'All Of You', 'Easter Parade', 'Three Little Words', 'Triplets', 'Steppin' Out With My Baby', 'A Couple Of Swells', 'Bouncin' The Blues', 'Three Little Words'. New numbers: 'That's Entertainment Part II', 'Be A Clown', 'Shubert Alley', 'Cartoon Sequence'. Metrocolor.

The Amazing Dobermans 1976 Doberman Associates/Golden Films. Director: Byron Chudnow. Producer: David Chudnow. *Stars*: James Franciscus, Barbara Eden, Fred Astaire, Jack Carter, Charlie Bill. Colour.

Un Taxi Mauve/The Purple Taxi 1977. Sofracima/Rizzoli Films. Director: Yves Boisset. Producers: Catherine Winter, Gisele Rebillion. *Stars*: Charlotte Rampling, Philippe Noiret, Agostina Belli, Peter Ustinov, Fred Astaire. Eastmancolor.

Ghost Story 1981. Universal. Director: John Irvin. Producer: Burt Weissbourd. *Stars*: Fred Astaire, Melvyn Douglas, Douglas Fairbanks Jr, John Houseman, Craig Wasson, Patricia Neal, Alice Krige. Technicolor.

PIBLIOGRAPHY

Astaire, Fred *Steps In Time* (New York, Harper, 1959)

Carrick, Peter *A Tribute To Fred Astaire* (London, Robert Hale, 1984)

Croce, Arlene *The Fred Astaire And Ginger Rogers Book* (New York, Galahad Books, 1972)

Dickens, Homer *The Films Of Ginger Rogers* (New Jersey, Secaucus, 1975)

Fordin, Hugh *The World Of Entertainment* (New York, Doubleday, 1975)

Freedland, Michael *Fred Astaire* (London, W.H. Allen 1976)

Green, Benny *Fred Astaire* (London, Hamlyn, 1979 New York, Exeter Books, 1979)

Jewell, Richard B. and Harbin, Vernon *The RKO Story* (London, Octopus, 1982)

McVay, Douglas *The Musical Film*, (A. Zwemmer, London A.S. Barnes, New York, 1967)

Parish, James Robert and Mank, Gregory *The Best of MGM: The Golden Years, 1928–1959* (New York, Arlington House, 1981)

Thomas, Bob *Fred Astaire, The Man, The Dancer* (London, Weidenfeld & Nicolson, 1985)

The Fred Astaire Story, His Life, His Films, His Friends (London, BBC Publications, 1975)

INDEX

191